THE
BOSTON
RED SOX

by
DONALD
HONIG

AN ILLUSTRATED TRIBUTE

ST. MARTIN'S PRESS · NEW YORK

Design by Holly Johnson at the Angelica Design
Group, Ltd.

Library of Congress Cataloging in Publication Data
Honig, Donald.
    The Boston Red Sox.
    1. Boston Red (Baseball team)—History.   I. Title.
GV875.B62H66 1984 796.357′64′0974461 83-19260
ISBN 0-312-09317-9

First Edition

10 9 8 7 6 5 4 3 2 1

For My Daughter Catherine

CONTENTS

ACKNOWLEDGMENTS

I AM DEEPLY INDEBTED to a number of people for their generous assistance in photo research and help in gathering the photographs reproduced in this book. Special thanks go to Michael P. Aronstein, president of the Card Memorabilia Associates, Ltd., in Amawalk, New York, and his son Andrew for their help and wisdom. Another great measure of appreciation must be expressed to George Sullivan, Public Relations Director of the Boston Red Sox, whose generous cooperation made a fellow writer's work so much easier. Thanks, too, to Bob Wood, Jack Redding, and those Red Sox players who allowed the use of pictures from their personal albums. The remaining photographs are from the following sources: J.J. Donnelly, Pearl River, New York: 260, 263, 266, 268, 276, 281, 282; Nancy Hogue, Warren, Ohio: 269, 274, 277, 278, 282, 283, 284, 285, 287, 288, 289, 290, 291, 292, 293, 296, 297. The photo on page 165 is from UPI.

Also, for their advice and guidance, a word of thanks to the following: Stanley Honig, Lawrence Ritter, David Markson, Allan Grotheer, Louis Kiefer, Mary E. Gallagher, Douglas Mulcahy, Joan Raines, Andrew Aronstein, and George Toporcer.

1 · A TEAM FOR ALL NEW ENGLAND

NO OTHER BASEBALL TEAM has fit into so neat a geographical package as the Boston Red Sox. No other part of the country has so sharply defined its character and characteristics as New England. With their lineage and their sense of history, New Englanders are proud and possessive, with a reputation for being taciturn and undemonstrative. But not even this legendary reserve can resist the wayward charm of their Huck Finn ball club, which has caused them so much exasperation and dejection, as well as occasional tinglings of elation and uproars of jubilation that have rent the sky over that Mecca known as Fenway Park, which when considered comparatively is perhaps the world's largest antique.

Like no other baseball team, the Boston Red Sox represents for its devotees not just a rooting interest and an emotion, but a vent for partisanship amounting in fervor almost to patriotism. It is part of the ongoing patrimony of New England, an heirloom of the heart, passed from one generation to the next, with shareholders living from the noiseless Maine woods to the reflective bowers of New Haven, from the reticence of Vermont villages to the industrial towns of Massachusetts and Connecticut, from New Hampshire's granite walls and Rhode Island's fisherman's coast to the sleek affluence of Connecticut's Fairfield County. To Maine lobstermen and Berkshire innkeepers and Cambridge intellectuals, they are known as "The Sox," loved and reviled, praised and damned by a fandom whose faith, fidelity, and capacity for forgiveness border on the saintly, unrivaled anywhere in that staunch, quaint, singularly American universe known as Baseball.

It all started in the mind of a tough, vain, arrogant, determinedly ambitious man named Byron Bancroft Johnson, known to everyone as Ban and to his enemies by other, more choice, names. And enemies he had. Ban Johnson had a view of the world and his place in it that lay fixed in his mind without a degree of modification or compromise. In context, the arrows of his aspirations were aimed at the summit and not an inch below. Ban Johnson's kind of ambition can be called admirable and noble; when impeded or confronted, it is often called ruthless. Johnson, equipped with a quality of self-confidence that seemed to thrive on confrontation the way a blade thrives on a whetstone, was the kind of man who probably took the word "ruthless" to be a compliment.

Ban Johnson was born in Norwalk, Ohio, in 1864, growing up in a world that seems to us today intolerable and unlivable. There was no automobile, no airplane, no television, and only one major league. Leaving the internal combustion engine, the lighter-than-air contraption, and the cathode tube to more mundane minds, Ban took upon himself the serious business of creating a second major league, one that would be stable and enduring (as several early pretenders had not).

Johnson was president of a circuit called the Western League. The fact that his outfit was considered the top minor league was not enough for Ban. He was out to put his confection of clubs on an equal footing with the National League, in the 1890s a twelve-team conglomeration with a monopoly on major league status.

Appropriately enough, Johnson organized his league just as the century was turning, the brand-new American League taking to the field for its first season in 1901. The charter

1

members were Chicago, Detroit, Milwaukee, and Cleveland in the west; Philadelphia, Baltimore, Washington, and Boston in the east. (In 1902 St. Louis replaced Milwaukee and in 1903 New York replaced Baltimore.)

Johnson wasn't just declaring his Western League as major; the tough, uncompromising Ohioan was doing it in full challenge to the long-established National League by putting teams in three of the latter's cities—Philadelphia, Chicago, and Boston—and by 1903, with the addition of St. Louis and New York, the two major leagues would be in head-to-head competition in five of their eight cities.

Boston, of course, was not virgin ground as far as big league ball was concerned. When the National League was formed in 1876, Boston was a charter member. Originally known as the Red Stockings, they later acquired the nickname "Beaneaters." The club was no small beans either, winning the National League pennant in 1891, 1892, 1893, 1897, and 1898. Playing on these championship Boston clubs were such outstanding performers as first baseman Fred Tenney, outfielder Chick Stahl, and third baseman Jimmy Collins, whom a half-century later certain senior citizens continued to insist was the all-time great at the position.

So Ban Johnson had his major league and he had his cities selected. What he needed now were players, and, more than anything else, he needed star players, both to give his operation credibility and to bring fans to the ticket booths. He could confer whatever status he wanted upon his league; without top-name ballplayers he was just blowing so much smoke.

There was no secret about where those players were—they were in the National League, each and every one of them with a signed contract. But those were heady days; American business ethics were still under the impact of the robber barons who had bribed and pillaged and exploited, and those contracts meant no more to Johnson than did last week's newspapers. The formidable president of the fledgling major league took on the established, monopolistic National League and whipped them in no time flat.

Once Ban's well-heeled club owners began scenting the air with the perfume of fresh money, player loyalties and contractual obligations started melting like April snow. Secure in their monopoly, the National League moguls were running their shop with a predictably tight-fisted grip. They had decreed a $2,400 salary ceiling for their hirelings, among whom were .400 hitters and 30-game winners, names like Wee Willie Keeler, Cy Young, Nap Lajoie, Ed Delahanty—a veritable marshaling of founding fathers of modern baseball history.

Unsurprisingly, the National League found no charity in its heart for the new league. There were mutterings, curses, bombast, threats, law suits, and countersuits. There was confusion, with some players bouncing back and forth between the leagues, depending on what tune was being played on whose cash register.

Fortunately for the Red Sox, who for their first decade or so were known as the "Pilgrims," their first owner was a real moneybags named Charles Somers. Somers had made his pile in the hearty areas of shipping, coal, and lumber, and he was only too happy to share some of his good fortune with the baseball-playing fraternity.

If curious Boston fans were wondering just how serious the new club in town was, they soon found out. In March 1901 it was announced that the Pilgrims had lured away from the Beaneaters the latter's splendid third baseman Jimmy Collins for a reported $4,000 per year contract (in those years a king's ransom, or at least a star third baseman's). By all accounts, Jimmy was the Brooks Robinson of the high-buttoned shoe era. It seems that he was particularly adept at coming in for bunts and throwing batters out at first base. This was no small potatoes in that dead-ball era when the bunt was a significant offensive weapon. In addition to his defensive razzle-dazzle, Jimmy was also a steady .300 hitter, and a choice specimen around whom to build a franchise. Thirty years old at the time, Collins was installed as the team's first manager.

The Beaneaters also saw their roster stripped of outfielder Chick Stahl, a solid performer who had averaged around .328 for his four years in their outfield. Another Beaneater who succumbed to the lure of the long green and jumped to the new team was outfielder-first

Ban Johnson

Lou Criger, Cy Young's favorite catcher.

Jimmy Collins

baseman Buck Freeman, the National League's home run champ in 1899 and a .300 hitter in 1900.

Collins probably spoke for his mates when he told the press, "I like to play baseball, but this is a business for me and I can't begoverned by sentiment." Jimmy's forthright words, in fact, need not be altered for any of today's players. Today, sentiment comes through the turnstiles, not the players' entrance.

The new club's biggest coup, however, came when they signed to a contract the game's premier pitcher, already a legendary performer, and even today one of the few mythic names of the baseball pantheon. He was a tall, sturdily built right-hander named Denton True Young whom everyone called "Cy," short for his original nickname of "Cyclone," bestowed in tribute to the speed of his fastball. Cy may or may not have been baseball's greatest pitcher, but the very fact that he is in the running for the distinction speaks for itself.

In 1901 Cy was thirty-four years old and had been pitching in the National League since 1890, first with Cleveland and then with St. Louis. After going 9–7 in his rookie year, he had won 20 or more for ten consecutive seasons, with highs of 36 in 1892, 32 in 1893, and 35 in 1895. Pitchers worked with greater frequency in those years and Cy's win totals were not considered extraordinary (neither his 36 nor 32 victories led the league). What Cy had to go along with his famous fastball and superb control was durability. During his twenty-two-year career he put in fifteen consecutive seasons of over, in most cases well over, 300 innings of work. He never had a sore arm, or if

he did, it was in the winter. He must have been one of the most remarkable physical specimens ever to make his living on a ball field.

It was because Cy was unhappy pitching in St. Louis—the summer heat there was not to the liking of this Ohio farmboy—that he let himself be wooed over to Ban Johnson's Boston outpost. It was a combination of the St. Louis heat, Johnson's persuasiveness, and the pulsebeat of a $3,500 contract that got Cy Young aboard the new Mayflower to join the latest Pilgrims. There was a bit of sour grapes on the part of the National League people as they watched their star pitcher depart to the competition. Some of the club owners said that Cy might have a good year in the new league because of the watered-down competition, but that would be about it because he was, after all, thirty-four years old.

Along with Cy came his favorite batterymate, catcher Lou Criger, who had been bruising his fingers on Cy's fast ones in both Cleveland and St. Louis since 1896.

One might say that the pattern of Boston Red Sox history was set in the club's first year, 1901. There was a spirited race for the pennant, some muscular hitting, a late-season pitching collapse, and a highly respectable but disappointing second-place finish. There was also, from the very beginning, the establishment of another Boston Red Sox trademark—a lively and devoted following. The new team drew just under 290,000 customers, second-best attendance figure in the league; but more important, they outdrew their National League rivals by a 2-to-1 ratio.

3

The Red Sox were from the very beginning the favored club in town, enjoying so thorough a monopoly on fan affection that the Boston Braves finally gave up trying to compete and in 1953 left town and took up residence in Milwaukee (on their way, eventually, to Atlanta).

Cy Young was seldom better than in that 1901 season. He rang up a 33– 10 season, leading the league in victories, earned run average (1.63), strikeouts (158), and shutouts (5). The Ohio farmboy also knew where he was putting the ball, walking just 37 men in 371 innings, as neat a one-in-ten average as you can get. If there had been a Cy Young Award in 1901, it would have gone to Cy Young.

But Cy couldn't do it alone. The only other pitcher on the club to end up over .500 was right-hander George Winter, 16–12.

The Red Sox were a hitting team from their inception. First baseman Buck Freeman batted .339, third best in the league. His 12 home runs were second to Nat Lajoie's 14 and his 114 runs batted in also ran him second to Nap's 125. Buck qualifies as the first in a long, long line of Red Sox power hitters, 12 homers being pretty hot stuff in those dead-ball days.

Manager Collins was right up there with a .332 batting average, followed by Chick Stahl's .309 and shortstop Freddy Parent's .306. Behind this steady hitting, and Cy Young's mighty right arm, the team battled the Chicago White Sox throughout the summer for the top rung, faltering toward the end and finishing four games out.

The American League played a 138-game schedule those first few years (which makes Young's 33 wins even more impressive), the 154-game season not coming along until 1904. Also, in that era pitchers were expected to finish what they started. Most staffs consisted of no more than five men; the day of the relief specialist was still far down the road. Young started 41 games and completed 38, Winter completed 26 of 28 starts, and righty Ted Lewis 31 of 34. The team as a whole had 123 complete games that season, second to Philadelphia's 124.

In 1902 the Pilgrims strengthened themselves on the mound by luring another Beaneater over to their side of town. He was a big,

twenty-six-year-old right-hander named Bill Dinneen who had been pitching in the National League since 1898. Dinneen, destined to have some moments of high glory during his five-year tenure with the club, broke in with a break-even 21–21 record.

Cy Young turned in a 32–10 record, again leading the team to a respectable showing, a third-place finish 6½ behind the Athletics as Connie Mack won his first pennant.

Collins' team added the bat of outfielder Patsy Dougherty to the lineup and Patsy made a solid debut with a .342 batting average. Collins had a .300-hitting outfield, for in addition to Dougherty, Chick Stahl swung away to a .323 mark and Freeman batted .309. Buck, the league's RBI leader with 121, had been moved to the outfield to make way for new first baseman Candy LaChance. Skipper Collins himself batted .322, giving the regular lineup four .300 sticks. But it wasn't enough, and again the finger of guilt pointed toward the mound. Young won 32, Dinneen 21, the rest of the staff 24.

A year later, in 1903, the team found the extra pitching they had been lacking, put together a solid, year-long effort and brought Boston its first American League pennant, winning in a romp over the Athletics by a 14½-game margin.

Buck Freeman supplied the power, leading the league with 13 home runs and 104 runs batted in. Dougherty gave the club another top year with the bat with a .331 average, while Freddie Parent hit .304 and Collins .296. The team was by far the most potent offensive force in the league, leading in batting, slugging, home runs, triples, hits, and runs. Their 48 home runs, a year's work for a single husky today, was good enough to stand as a league record until 1920 and the lively ball era.

The Boston mound staff featured three 20-game winners in that first, long-ago pennant season. Cy Young did not win 30, but his 28– 9 record gave him the league lead in wins for the third straight year. Cy certainly was giving the team its money's worth—for his first three years his record was 93–29, which is the way to pitch if you want to have an award named after you. Bill Dinneen was 21–12. The new man, the one who made the difference, was a tall right-hander named Long Tom Hughes. Long Tom had been picked up the year before from Baltimore but had contributed little because of a tender arm. In 1903, however, his only full season with Boston (he was dealt to New York the next year), Hughes was 20–7.

Also a one-year resident of Boston in 1903 was the team's new owner, Henry J. Killilea, a Milwaukee attorney who had bought out Charles Somers. Henry's tenure in town may have been brief, but it was eminently satisfying and historically significant, for he helped launch what has become America's most extravagant sporting event, one that cannot be overcooked or served too richly, despite all attempts to do so.

The American League was in its third year now, having silenced the skeptics and disappointed the ill-wishers. With the new league solidly established, and with the raiding of each other's rosters brought to a halt by agreement, fans and sportswriters had begun agitating for a postseason series to be played between the respective pennant winners to crown a champion.

THE WORLD SERIES

The man who took the first step toward the creation of the World Series was the owner of the Pittsburgh Pirates, Barney Dreyfuss. With their clubs sailing toward pennants that year, Dreyfuss sat down one August afternoon and penned a letter to Killilea suggesting their two teams meet in a best-five-out-of-nine series to determine baseball's best team. Dreyfuss stressed both the public relations and financial advantage of such a series.

Killilea took up the matter with Ban Johnson. The American League president saw the possibilities and liked them. For the two pennant winners to meet on the same field would dispel once and for all any lingering notions that might be left concerning his league's equality with the National. And if the American League club could win such a series, all the better.

Dreyfuss' team was a good one, on its way to a third consecutive flag. The Pirates had strong pitching in Deacon Phillippe and Sam Leever and some outstanding players in player-

manager Fred Clarke, Ginger Beaumont, Tommy Leach, and their mighty shortstop Honus Wagner. Jimmy Collins was convinced that Young and Dinneen could beat the Pirate bats into cornstalks, and when Johnson heard this he gave Killilea the go ahead. "Play them," the autocrat of the American League said. "And beat them," he added. "You must beat them."

Boston went appropriately delirious at the thought of the World Series. In three short years the Pilgrims had inspired a following second to none in devotion, loyalty, and unbridled enthusiasm. Chief among these was a band known as "The Royal Rooters," who attended games with volume turned up high, cheering and yelling and singing songs and making music from an assortment of instruments. The evangelical fervor of these fans has been matched in charm and lunacy only by the customers at Brooklyn's old Ebbets Field some decades later.

The first three games of the first World Series were scheduled for Boston's Huntington Avenue Grounds, with the next four to be played in Pittsburgh, and the final two, if necessary, back in Boston.

The first game was played on October 1 with Young pitching against Phillippe. The Pirates got to Cy for four runs in the very first inning and went on from there to a 7–3 victory. The following day Dinneen squared things away with a 3–0 shutout. The hitting star of the day was Dougherty with two home runs. It was an eye-catching performance by Patsy, especially in light of the fact that he had popped only two homers all season long.

Phillippe came back with one day's rest in Game Three and beat Long Tom Hughes 4–2. Long Tom pitched just two innings before giving way to relief pitcher Cy Young. The series went eight games and aside from Hughes' two innings in the third game, every Boston pitch was thrown by either Young or Dinneen.

Pitching for the third time in six days, Phillippe edged Dinneen in Game Four, putting Pittsburgh ahead three games to one. The next day, Young put Boston back in it with an 11–2 win. Dinneen evened things up at three games apiece with a 6–3 win in Game Six, beating

Leever, who was suffering from a sore arm throughout the series.

Young defeated Phillippe in the final game at Pittsburgh by a 7–3 score, pinning a loss on the Deacon after three straight wins. That was on October 10. On October 13, back in Boston, Dinneen scored his third win when he shut out Phillippe and the Pirates 3–0, giving Boston the series and making them "world champions."

Artistically and financially, the first World Series had to be counted a success, particularly in the view of Ban Johnson. The Boston victory had confirmed beyond any further doubt that his league had coequal status with the National. If the Boston players won the championship, however, the Pirate players came away from the affair with fatter checks. To salve his players' feelings, Barney Dreyfuss threw his owner's share into the pot, allowing each of his men to receive a check of $1,316. Boston owner Killilea, behaving as an owner, kept his share (it amounted to around $6,700), so that his players each received a winner's share of $1,182. It remains the only time in World Series history that the losers were better paid than the winners.

Killilea not only pocketed his winnings, he ran with them. After batting 1.000 as an owner—one year, one pennant, one world championship—Henry Killilea sold out and disappeared from the baseball scene.

The third owner of the Boston Pilgrims in five years was General Charles Henry Taylor, owner, publisher, and editor of the *Boston Globe* and one of the city's sterling citizens. The general's purpose in buying the ball club was to provide a diversion for his son, John I. Taylor. The younger Taylor had built for himself a reputation as a playboy and high-living sportsman. The Pilgrims would not only be fun to own, but they were also a very sound business investment. When Killilea put the club up for sale there was no lack of willing buyers. Among the men Taylor outbid was John F. "Honey Fitz" Fitzgerald, later one of Boston's legendary mayors and grandfather of President John F. Kennedy.

John I. Taylor's first year of ownership was a memorable one, as the Pilgrims wrapped themselves up in a pennant race that remains one of the most dramatic in American League history. Not only did the club win a second straight flag, but they were a resounding financial success—drawing nearly 625,000 paid admissions, quite a sizable number in those days. To indicate the dimensions of that attendance, one need only take a look at how long it took other American League clubs to do as well. In took the Browns until 1922 to top Boston's figure, Cleveland 1920, Detroit 1919, Washington 1925, the Yankees 1919. Only the White Sox and Athletics topped the Boston figure in a few years' time, while Boston topped itself only once before 1936.

On May 5 that year the thirty-seven-year-old Cy Young pitched the twentieth century's first perfect game when he "skunked" (that's the way the papers said it) Connie Mack's A's 3–0. Cy's victim was the A's left-handed fireballer Rube Waddell, who four days earlier, in the opener of a five-game series, one-hit the Pilgrims in beating Jesse Tannehill. Rube, who could blather as well as he could pitch, nearly had a perfecto himself—he yielded a single to the leadoff man and then put away the next twenty-seven men in a row. Before Young and Waddell hooked up four days later, Waddell reportedly yelled at old Cy, "I'll give you the same thing I gave Tannehill the other day." Thusly provoked, or inspired, Young gave Rube the most eloquent answer possible, leaving the final word to Connie Mack, who shook his head and said, "I have never seen such a game pitched," nor was he ever to witness another like it, though he remained in baseball for another forty-six years.

Tannehill turned in his own nifty on August 17, delivering a no-hitter against the White Sox. Jesse, acquired from New York in a swap for Long Tom Hughes, gave the Pilgrims a fine year with a 21–11 record. Tannehill, the first lefty the team ever had in the regular rotation, backed up a 27–16 year by Young and a 23–14 showing by Dinneen, giving the club three 20-game winners for the second year in a row.

VICTORY ON THE LAST DAY

It was the first of many pulsing pennant races the team would run with their rivals from New York, then known as the Highlanders. The New Yorkers had a one-man band on the mound that year, a right-handed spitballer named Jack Chesbro, who set the modern record for wins with a 41–12 season. Chesbro started 51 games, completed 48, pitched 455 innings, and logged a 1.82 ERA. It was an incredible, Herculean year-long effort, and it all went down the drain with a single pitch on the last day of the season.

Three times in history the Boston and the New York American League clubs were destined to go to the season's finale to determine the pennant—in 1904, 1949, and 1978. In 1904 the palm went to Boston.

The Pilgrims came to play at New York's Hilltop Park on October 10, a game-and-a-half up with a twin bill on tap. Boston needed just one win to walk off with their second straight flag. The opener saw the ubiquitous Chesbro matched against Dinneen. True to the script that these two clubs would adhere to in their later fateful meetings, the opener went into the ninth inning in a tense 2–2 tie. In the top of the ninth Lou Criger, a modest .211 hitter that year, led off and singled, the most momentous hit of his sixteen-year career. A sacrifice and a ground out moved Lou around to third.

It was now that Chesbro, working his 455th and last inning of the year, wound up and put everything he had on the ball. He put too much. The errant delivery sailed over catcher Red Kleinow's head and Criger ran across the plate with what proved to be the pennant-winning run, on history's most famous wild pitch. Dinneen put the Highlanders away in the bottom of the ninth and the Royal Rooters, down in force from Boston to watch it all happen, broke out their musical instruments and began a celebration that ended with a torchlight parade down Broadway that night.

For Boston fans of later years, doomed to watch powerhouse clubs sink under the waves due to lack of good pitching, that 1904 staff is enough to make them misty-eyed. The club carried just five pitchers all year: Young, Dinneen, Tannehill, Norwood Gibson, and George Winter, and they turned in a collective 2.12 earned run average. They also rang up another eye-catching statistic—148 complete games, still the major league record.

Thanks to the New York Giants' manager John J. McGraw, there was no World Series that year. McGraw, who nursed his grudges as assiduously as a mother with a suckling babe, didn't like Ban Johnson and refused to let his pennant-winning Giants meet the Pilgrims in a postseason contest, unwilling to lend more prestige to Johnson's league.

McGraw's pigheadedness pleased no one, least of all his own players, who winced at the thought of the extra loot—around $1,500 per man, a highly noticeable sum of money back then—flying out of their pockets. The uproar from the press and fans, who had been looking forward to another World Series, was so vociferous that even the dictatorial Mr. McGraw had to pay attention. The World Series resumed the next year (with McGraw's Giants as coparticipants) and has continued on without interruption, despite two world wars, a depression, and John McGraw.

The 1904 season marked the pinnacle of the team's success in its first decade. They dropped to fourth place in 1905 and a year later took a dive to the cellar with a 49–105 record. Now the problem was hitting. In 1905 they hit .234, a year later .239. And even Cy Young was proving to be mortal, dropping to 17–19 in 1905 and 13–21 the next year.

The '06 club had the bleak distinction of setting a league record for consecutive losses that still stands—20. Making it all the more embarrassing, 19 of those losers came when the club was on display at their Huntington Avenue Grounds home. The man who more than any other came to epitomize the mortifying '06 season was a twenty-four-year-old right-hander named Joe Harris. Young Joe suffered through a 3–21 purgatory. He did have his moments, however. On September 1 he pitched 24 innings against the Athletics and lost 4–1, giving up three runs in the top of the 24th after shutting out the A's for 20 consecutive innings. (The 24 innings remains in the books as the longest game ever in the American League.) Joe came back for more the next year, but after running up an 0–6 record the club decided to cash him in. Joe Harris departed, leaving behind a lifetime 4–29 record.

Also outward bound was manager Jimmy Collins. The skipper wasn't getting along with owner Taylor and by August the two weren't speaking. Jimmy resigned as manager, though remaining as the team's third baseman until early the following season, when he was dealt to the A's. The new manager was outfielder Chick Stahl.

Stahl's reign as manager was brief, tragically terminated during spring training in 1907. The thirty-four-year-old skipper injured his leg and was given a solution of carbolic acid and water for use as treatment. For some inexplicable reason, he drank it. An hour later he was dead. No satisfactory explanation has ever been advanced for Chick Stahl's suicide. He was a deeply religious man, happily married, and by all accounts untroubled and content.

The 1907 club, now officially rechristened the Red Sox by Taylor, sleep-walked through the season under the guidance of four different managers. Cy Young, who did not want the job, ran the club for a week or so until a new man could be hired. His name was George Huff, a scout for the Chicago Cubs. George lasted for all of eight games, whereupon Taylor decided Huff was a mistake and canned him. First baseman Bob Unglaub was next and Bob wrote out the lineup for 26 games, lost 20 of them, and became a first baseman exclusively again. The year's fourth manager was Jim (Deacon) McGuire, as grizzled a veteran as there was. The forty-four-year-old Deacon, a catcher, had been in the big leagues since 1884. Deacon guided the hapless Red Sox to a seventh-place finish, got them up to sixth the next year, and then was given the boot in August. The next man was Fred Lake, who lasted through the 1909 season, finished third, and was fired.

The cast was changing now. Dinneen was gone and so was Tannehill. And after the 1908 season, during which he hurled his third no-hitter at the age of forty-one, 21-game winner Cy Young was sold to Cleveland for $12,500.

By the end of the 1909 season, not one player from the 1904–05 pennant winners remained. The Red Sox were the youngest team in the league and some of the talent that was to make the upcoming decade the most successful in Red Sox history was already in place. Chief among them were a nineteen-year-old right-hander with a blinding fastball named Smoky Joe Wood, outfielders Tris Speaker and Harry Hooper, and a rugged catcher with leadership abilities named Bill (Rough) Carrigan. And at a school for wayward boys in Baltimore was a headstrong, untamed fifteen-year-old named George Herman Ruth who was beginning to flex the athletic muscles that would soon make him the most spectacular performer in the game's history.

Cy Young

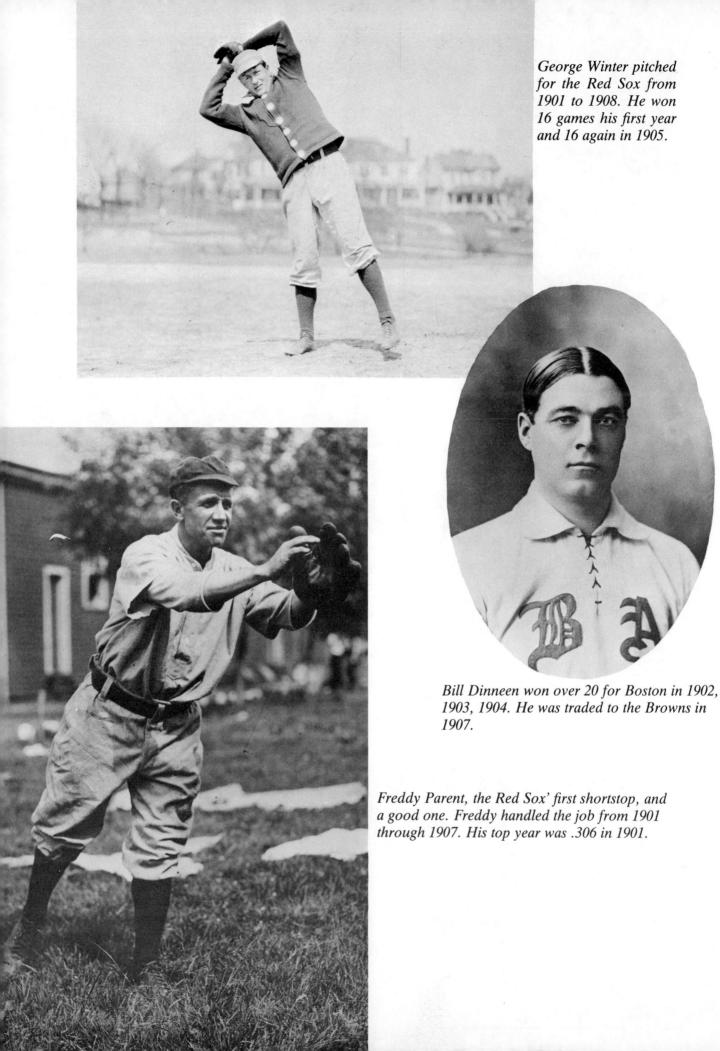

George Winter pitched for the Red Sox from 1901 to 1908. He won 16 games his first year and 16 again in 1905.

Bill Dinneen won over 20 for Boston in 1902, 1903, 1904. He was traded to the Browns in 1907.

Freddy Parent, the Red Sox' first shortstop, and a good one. Freddy handled the job from 1901 through 1907. His top year was .306 in 1901.

Patsy Dougherty. The popular outfielder batted .342 and .331 before being swapped to New York in 1904.

The Huntington Avenue Grounds before one of the games against Pittsburgh in the 1903 World Series.

A shot of the Boston dugout during the 1903
World Series. The man at the far left is Cy
Young.

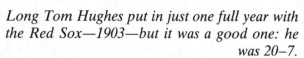
Long Tom Hughes put in just one full year with
the Red Sox—1903—but it was a good one: he
was 20–7.

George (Candy) LaChance, Red Sox first baseman from 1902 to 1905.

Jesse Tannehill, Boston's first left-handed ace. He pitched for them from 1904 to 1908, winning 21 in 1904 and again the next year.

Bob Unglaub, first baseman with Boston from 1904 to 1908, who also managed briefly in 1907.

Above: Norwood Gibson, who pitched for Boston from 1903 to 1906. He was a 17-game winner in 1904.

Below: Pitcher Joe Harris, who lost all those games in 1906.

Chick Stahl

The first infield. Left to right: *Jimmy Collins, Freddy Parent, Hobe Ferris, Buck Freeman.*

Above: Deacon McGuire, shown here when he was managing Cleveland in 1909, a year after he was let out as Red Sox skipper.

Below: Kip Selbach, outfielder with the Red Sox from 1904 to 1906.

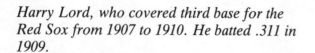

Harry Lord, who covered third base for the Red Sox from 1907 to 1910. He batted .311 in 1909.

Fred Lake, Red Sox manager in 1908 and 1909.

Cy Morgan pitched for the Red Sox from 1907 to 1909, when he was traded to the Athletics. He won 13 for the Sox in 1908.

2 · THE GREATEST YEARS

TRIS SPEAKER FIRST JOINED the Red Sox in 1907 at the age of nineteen. He got into 7 games that year, 31 the next. In 1909 the young Texan took over as the team's regular center fielder, a position he played with such immaculate skill and ease that he soon became the standard by which a generation of center fielders was judged. In that dead-ball era an outfielder could play shallower than they do today, but Speaker played so shallow that he was able on occasion to turn in unassisted double plays and get involved in rundowns. He possessed top running speed and the unerring instincts that all superior athletes must have. His contemporaries claim that very few balls were ever hit over his head. In addition, this most complete of baseball players had a throwing arm so strong that he set still-standing records for assists.

And he could hit. Beginning with his first full year in 1909, Speaker batted .300 or better in eighteen of nineteen seasons, eleven times batting .340 or better, five times going over .380. Destined to be overshadowed by the more mercurial and charismatic Ty Cobb, Tris nevertheless wrote some enduring records of his own. Chief among his offensive achievements is the distinction of being the most prolific producer of two-base hits. He holds the American League record for leading in doubles, eight times, and is the all-time champ in that department with a lifetime total of 793.

Also playing his first full year in 1910 was twenty-two-year-old right fielder Harry Hooper, a man whose defensive prowess was said to equal Speaker's. Though not as potent at the plate as Speaker—few men were—Harry swung a steady .280 bat. Hooper is remembered the way any athlete would prefer to

be—as a man who played inspired ball in the clutch, whether it was getting a base hit when it counted most or finding that extra leg of speed and making the acrobatic, game-saving catch.

The third member of what is still generally regarded as the all-time Red Sox outfield was George (Duffy) Lewis. Duffy was just twenty-two when he showed up in Boston in 1910 and immediately put an armlock on left field. Another excellent glove, he kept his batting averages in the .280s and was, one of his teammates recalled admiringly, "a swell guy when the chips were down."

The Red Sox were building a fine mound corps in 1910. Manager Patsy Donovan had right-handers Eddie Cicotte, Charley Hall, Joe Wood, and lefty Ray Collins. Cicotte was traded to the White Sox two years later and became one of the league's best until caught up in the scandalous 1919 World Series. Eddie was one of the chief conspirators in that dismal episode. Hall and Collins had some winning seasons for the Red Sox, but the jewel of the staff was young Wood, all of twenty years old in 1910 and already acclaimed as one of the hardest throwers in baseball, one of the few whose swifty was said to measure up to the lightning bolt unleashed by Walter Johnson.

The Red Sox bought the baby-faced Wood from Kansas City of the American Association in August 1908. It was Cy Young's last year with the team and in an interview some seventy years later Joe Wood recalled Young and Walter Johnson. "Cy was around forty years old at the time I joined the club, but I don't think you could say he was over the hill since he pitched three hundred innings that year and won 21 games. No, he didn't pay much attention to me. I don't think we talked to one another at all. I was just an unknown kid coming onto the club and Cy Young was the greatest pitcher of his day. I don't suppose there are many people alive today who saw him in his heyday, but for a long time it was said he was the greatest pitcher who ever lived. I don't know how you measure those things; I guess each generation has its candidate for the greatest this or the greatest that. As far as I'm concerned, Walter Johnson was the greatest pitcher that ever lived. I just never saw anyone else who had as much natural ability. He could throw the ball by you so fast you never knew whether you'd swung under it or over it."

A few years after Wood's arrival, when Johnson was asked if he could throw harder than Wood, Johnson replied, "Listen, my friend, there's no man alive can throw harder than Smoky Joe Wood."

In 1909, his first full season, young Joe Wood was 11–8. In 1910 he was 12–13 with a 1.68 ERA. In 1911, poised on the brink of breathtaking greatness, the handsome youngster was 23–17 with a 2.02 ERA.

In 1911, a year before the greatest winning season in Red Sox history, the club finished fifth. But they were ready now to unseat a powerful Philadelphia Athletics club that had taken pennants in 1910 and 1911. It was perhaps the grandest Red Sox year ever, that 1912 season. Not only did the team set a league record with 105 wins (it stood until the 1927 Yankees won 110), not only did they have a pitcher who won 34 games (Wood) and an outfielder who batted .383 (Speaker), not only did they win one of the most exciting World Series ever, but they did it in a brand-new ball park.

THE SOX FIND A HOME: FENWAY PARK

There are certain baseball verities that may come as gentle shocks to certain of today's fans. Connie Mack was once a young man. Baseball players were once underpaid. The Boston Red Sox didn't always play in Fenway Park.

The team's first home was a park with wooden grandstands built on Huntington Avenue, on a site now occupied by Northeastern University. The Huntington Avenue Grounds, as the new ball park was known, accommodated around 7,000 people in its modest wooden stands, with room for a few thousand more in the outfield. The field was home to the Boston American League club until the building of Fenway Park in 1912. In 1911, a year before he sold the club to former big league ballplayer and manager Jimmy McAleer, John I. Taylor authorized the construction of a new home for his team. What rose at the corner of Landsdowne and Jersey Streets was Fenway Park, a small, intimate, slightly misshapen ball yard that has become the Mecca of Red Sox fans and with the passage of time a place where baseball history is fairly palpable, a shimmering presence that can evoke the shadows of the game's most burnished names.

The most famous feature of Fenway Park is its notorious left field wall, "The Green Monster." It is but 315 feet down the line to this beckoning target, which is 37 feet from base to top. Later, a 23-foot netting was added. Balls hit into the net are home runs; off the wall is all you can get, making Fenway the home of the double and the long single.

Interestingly enough, when Fenway opened and fans got a look at the tall barrier in left field, there was some skepticism about anybody clouting a ball over it—this was still the dead-ball era of course. And as a matter of fact, Boston's home run production dropped considerably after they moved into Fenway. In their last three years at the Huntington Avenue Grounds they averaged 33 homers a year; for their first three seasons in Fenway they averaged 21.

The team also unveiled a new manager in 1912. He was Jake Stahl, younger brother of the late Chick. This remains the only instance in big league history of two brothers having managed the same team. Jake had played briefly for the Red Sox in 1903, then gone on to become player-manager for Washington in 1905–06, when he was just twenty-six years old. After being swapped to the Yankees, Jake rejoined the Sox in 1908 and became their regular first baseman. In 1910 he led the league with 10 home runs.

The rest of the 1912 team included third

baseman Larry Gardner, who held down that position from 1910 through 1917; Steve Yerkes at second, Charles (Heinie) Wagner at short, and Bill Carrigan behind the plate. The outfield was, of course, Hooper, Speaker, and Lewis.

Behind Wood, who was 34–5 that year, was Hugh Bedient with an 18–9 rookie year, Buck O'Brien 19–13, Charley Hall 15–8, and Ray Collins, the only lefty on the staff, 15–8.

Joe Wood's season was arguably the greatest enjoyed by a pitcher in the twentieth century, with Walter Johnson's 1913 season of 36–7 perhaps the only one better. Wood, a superb all-around athlete (he batted .290 that year), struck out 258 batters, pitched 10 shutouts, had a 1.91 ERA, and completed 35 of 38 starts. He also faced Johnson in a game on September 6 that for sheer drama remains an absolute classic.

Earlier in the season Johnson, on the way to a 32–12 campaign, had set a new record by winning 16 straight games, his streak coming to an end on August 23. But the Washington speedballer had very little time to comfortably savor this latest of his many mound glories, for steaming along the very same tracks was Boston's Joe Wood. Smoky Joe was mowing down team after team with punishing regularity and soon was approaching the brand-new record.

On September 6 Wood was going after his 14th straight and the man he was facing at Fenway Park was Johnson himself. It was a match-up made in heaven. Years later Wood recalled the event in a conversation with Lawrence Ritter, published in Ritter's classic *The Glory of Their Times:*

"It was on a Friday. My regular pitching turn was scheduled to come on Saturday, and they moved it up a day so that Walter and I could face each other. Walter had already won sixteen in a row and his streak had ended. I had won thirteen in a row and they challenged our manager, Jake Stahl, to pitch me against Walter, so Walter could stop my streak himself. Jake agreed, and to match us against each other he moved me up in the rotation from Saturday to Friday.

"The newspapers publicized us like prize-fighters: giving statistics comparing our height, weight, biceps, triceps, arm span and whatnot.

The Champion, Walter Johnson, versus the Challenger, Joe Wood. That was the only game I ever remember in Fenway Park, or anywhere else for that matter, where the fans were sitting practically along the first-base and third-base lines. Instead of sitting back where the bench usually is, we were sitting on chairs right up against the foul lines, and the fans were right behind us. The overflow had been packed between the grandstand and foul lines, as well as out in the outfield behind ropes. Fenway Park must have contained twice as many people as its seating capacity that day. I never saw so many people in one place in my life. In fact, the fans were put on the field an hour before the game started, and it was so crowded down there I hardly had room to warm up."

The two titans of the mound did not disappoint expectations. It was pitching the crowd had come to see, a pitching they saw, as each man worked with the same scintillating efficiency they had displayed all summer long. The twenty-two-year-old Smoky Joe Wood and the twenty-four-year-old Walter Johnson exploded fastballs all afternoon, pitching to a 1–0 decision with the nod going to Wood. The Boston run came with two out in the sixth inning. Speaker doubled to left and Duffy Lewis followed a moment later with a two-bagger that fell along the right field line. Both hits went to the opposite field, meaning that Johnson was not easy to pull that day.

The victory was Wood's 14th in a row. He added two more, tying Johnson's record, before he was stopped by Detroit on September 20 by a 6–4 score. The record still stands in the American League, since tied by Philadelphia's Lefty Grove in 1931 and Detroit's Schoolboy Rowe in 1934.

It was the Red Sox versus the New York Giants in the 1912 World Series, and the cast of characters included Giants manager John McGraw and his long-time ace, Christy Mathewson, considered by many the mightiest of all pitchers.

Mathewson had begun to slow down just a bit after eleven years, meaning his record was 23–12, his ERA 2.12, his highest in five years. McGraw's ace that year was a tall, hard-throwing twenty-two-year-old southpaw named

Rube Marquard, who was 26–11. Behind these two was twenty-three-year-old spitballing right-hander, Jeff Teserau, 16–7 and the National League's ERA leader with a 1.96 mark.

In that year of individual winning streaks, Marquard had spun out one of his own, winning his first 19 games, still the all-time big league mark. But it was Mathewson who impressed young Joe Wood:

"I don't think he was as fast as he had once been," Wood recalled. "When I saw him his greatest asset was control and a beautiful curve ball that he'd start over your head and bring right down. I'd never seen a curve ball like it. He also threw what they called the fadeaway, which is the same as a screwball. As far as I know, he was the only one who threw it at that time."

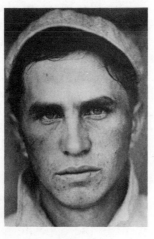

Harry Hooper, Boston's brilliant right fielder from 1909 to 1920. His best batting average for the Sox was .312 in 1920.

John I. Taylor   *Tris Speaker*

And what did young Joe Wood throw? "Fastball and curve. That's all there was to it. Didn't throw anything else."

McGraw surprised everyone when he bypassed both Mathewson and Marquard and opened the Series at the Polo Grounds with Teserau. There was no comparable surprise from Jake Stahl: It was Joe Wood.

Smoky Joe got the Sox off to a winning start, beating the Giants 4–3, but not after some deep breaths were drawn and held in the bottom of the ninth. The Giants had one run in and men on second and third with one out, Art Fletcher and Doc Crandall coming to bat. Young Joe, who had already fanned 9, made Fletcher his 10th victim, throwing so hard that he said, "I thought my arm would fly right off my body." Then he went to work on Crandall,

throwing fastballs, "just burning them in and hoping for the best." With a full count, Wood fired one past Crandall for his 11th strikeout and the ball game.

The next day the two clubs played to a 6–6 tie in 11 innings, called because of darkness. Five errors behind him undid Mathewson. The Red Sox used Collins, Hall, and Bedient. The next day Marquard tied the Series with a 2–1 win over Buck O'Brien. But then Wood put the Red Sox up by one again with a 3–1 win over Teserau. The Red Sox then took a commanding three games to one lead when Bedient outdueled Mathewson, 2–1.

With a world championship just one game away, Boston saw its lead evaporate in the next two games, losing 5–2 to Marquard and then 11–4 to Teserau as the Giants hammered Wood for seven hits and six runs in the first inning. The latter game was notable for a rather noisy and unpleasant fracas that broke out before a pitch was thrown.

"It seems," Joe Wood recalled, "that more tickets had been sold than there were seats, and it so happened that the people who were shut out were the Royal Rooters. Well, it took the mounted police to get them to go and when they finally did go they took part of the center field fence with them. I was all warmed up and ready to start pitching and then that crowd broke down the fence. I had to go and sit down on the bench until it was fixed. Some people said that was why I got hit so hard in the first inning, that I had cooled off. But I don't think that had anything to do with it."

So it boiled down to a final and deciding

game. McGraw had the grea Mathewson primed, while Stahl sent Bedient out for the Red Sox.

The Giants took a 1–0 lead in the top of the third and Mathewson nursed it along until the last of the seventh. The Sox got two men on and Stahl sent a little Danish-born reserve outfielder named Olaf Henrikson up to hit for Bedient. It was Olaf's one and only time at bat in the Series and he made it a good one, sending one of Mathewson's offerings down the left field line for a game-tying double.

Joe Wood took over for the Red Sox in the top of the eighth and for the next two innings the young Boston phenomenon and the veteran New York master dueled on even terms. Then came the tenth inning.

In the top of the tenth the Giants scored on

the dead run. Years later Hooper still remembered the catch with a mixture of admiration and chagrin. "Ninety-nine times out of a hundred no outfielder could possibly have come close to that ball," he said. "But in some way, I don't know how, Snodgrass ran like the wind, and dang if he didn't catch it."

Engle tagged up and went to third after the catch, the tying run.

After that, Steve Yerkes walked, and then came another critical mistake by the Giants. Speaker lifted a little pop foul between first and home. Joe Wood never forgot what happened. "The first baseman, Fred Merkle, had the best shot at it. But instead of calling for Merkle to take it, Mathewson came down off the mound calling for Chief Meyers, the catcher. Merkle could have caught it easily,

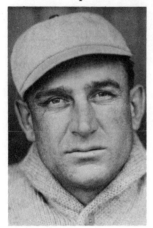

Jake Stahl

Smoky Joe Wood in 1911.

Duffy Lewis, the third member of Boston's famed World War 1–era outfield. Duffy played for the Red Sox from 1910 through 1917.

a double by Red Murray and a single by Fred Merkle. With their backs to the wall and Christy Mathewson on the mound, the Red Sox came to bat. Clyde Engle pinch-hit for Wood (who had injured his hand making the last out in the top of the inning) and lofted a soon-to-be-famous fly ball out to center where the usually sure-handed Fred Snodgrass waited for it to come down. The ball descended, struck Snodgrass' glove, and dropped to the grass. Engle ended up on second base.

Hooper was the next batter and Harry hit a shot that became a perfect demonstration of baseball irony. It was a line drive that looked like it was going to carry over Snodgrass' head in center. But now, in a complete reversal of form, Snodgrass raced back at top speed and made a spectacular over-the-shoulder catch on

but Mathewson kept calling for Meyers, I'll never know why. You see, Merkle was coming in on the ball and the Chief was going with it. It's a much easier play for Merkle. But there was Matty, yelling for the Chief. I can hear him to this day. But Meyers never could get to it. The ball dropped. It just clunked down into the grass in foul ground and lay there. We couldn't believe it. Neither could Mathewson. You never saw a man as mad as he was when that ball hit the ground. But the way we saw it, it was his own fault. He called for the wrong man."

With two large helpings from the Giants now, the Red Sox forged ahead. Speaker lined a single to right to tie the game. On the throw to third trying to get Yerkes, Speaker went to second. McGraw walked Duffy Lewis to fill the bases. Larry Gardner—"always a dependable fellow," said Wood—then hit a long fly to right to bring in the winning run, giving the Red Sox the championship.

The glory of 1912 was going to have to sustain Red Sox fans for a while; the club dropped to fourth place in 1913 as Connie Mack's A's won their third pennant in four years. The prime reason for Boston's descent was a broken thumb suffered in spring training by Joe Wood. Perhaps he tried to come back too soon, but whatever the reason, the hop was suddenly gone from that lethal fastball and Joe Wood's rainbow crumbled and came earthward. There were occasional flashes of past greatness for the next few years, but now they were the tail of the comet, leaving the handsome youngster frozen in baseball history with his 34–5 record, destined never to age on the pitching mound. Joe Wood's career remains the most tantalizing what-might-have-been in all of baseball. Only the injury-aborted careers of Brooklyn's Pete Reiser in the 1940s and Cleveland's Herb Score a decade later bear comparison to Joe Wood's in what the game was deprived of.

Without Wood, the staff had no leader, though lefty Ray Collins was 20–8, Bedient 16–14, and a newcomer, twenty-one-year-old left-hander Hubert (Dutch) Leonard, broke in with a 14–17 season. Speaker led a sputtering attack with a .365 average.

Midway through the season McAleer canned Jake Stahl—the two had been bickering for some time—and replaced him with the club's catcher, twenty-nine-year-old Bill Carrigan.

A 1907 graduate of Holy Cross, Carrigan had been nicknamed "Rough" when he joined the club. The Maine-born Irishman was quiet and a gentleman, but his pugnacious lantern jaw, gunfighter's eyes, and air of businesslike self-confidence proclaimed him a man not to be trifled with. Fair-minded but a disciplinarian, Carrigan quickly won the respect of his men. "He was tops," said pitcher Ernie Shore, who joined the club in 1914. "Best manager in the world."

After the 1913 season the team was sold again. The new owner was Joseph J. Lannin, a Quebec-born businessman who had made weighty sums of money operating in, among other things, New York City real estate. The price Lannin paid was around $200,000, or about what a .240 hitter earns today.

The A's repeated in 1914, with Carrigan moving his club up to second place, 8½ games out. There were a couple of key additions to the infield. A slick-fielding twenty-one-year-old rookie named Everett Scott took over at shortstop, while first baseman Dick Hoblitzell was a mid-season acquisition from the National League. Ray Collins won 20 again, his last productive season before a lame arm ended his career the following season. But the ace was Leonard with an 18–5 record and what is still the lowest earned run average in baseball history—1.01. Turning in a 14–8 record was right-hander George (Rube) Foster. Also up that year was young righty Ernie Shore, breaking in with a 9–4 record. Along with Leonard's historic ERA, Foster was 1.65 and Shore 1.99. The Sox were in those years coming up with a wealth of mound talent that could only make their fans of a later era sigh wistfully. The staff's 2.35 ERA and 26 shutouts were tops in the league.

Another pitcher made his big league debut for the Sox in 1914, a nineteen-year-old left-hander named George Herman (Babe) Ruth. The date was July 11, the place Fenway Park. The new man started and beat Cleveland, 4–3, although lifted for a pinch-hitter (Duffy Lewis) in the seventh. And so it began, the most resounding career in the history of baseball or any other sport.

George Herman Ruth was born on February 7, 1895, in a wooden frame house in Baltimore. By the turn of the century he was living upstairs from a saloon his father owned. The unruly, fun-loving, mischief-making nature that was to enchant fans, amuse sportswriters, and enrage managers was already evident by the time the boy was eight years old. A chronic truant, unresponsive to discipline, Ruth finally found himself turned over to St. Mary's school, an industrial school and home for troublesome youngsters. Although run by the Xaverian Brothers, a Catholic order, St. Mary's was nonsectarian, taking in boys of all denominations.

Along with a full regimen of classroom work and industrial training, St. Mary's encouraged athletic activity. A natural athlete, Ruth took part in football, basketball, and baseball. It was baseball that most fascinated the youngster, the game he was soon to conquer and make over in his own image.

By the time he was seventeen Ruth, still living at St. Mary's, had developed into an outstanding pitcher with a smoking fastball. He was seen by Jack Dunn, owner and manager of the Baltimore Orioles, then an independently owned club in the International League. After promising the Xaverians that he would not only be manager to Ruth but would also look out for the boy's personal wellbeing, Dunn signed him to pitch for Baltimore in 1914 at a salary of around $150 per month.

Ruth was an instant success. By the beginning of July he had already won 14 games for the Orioles. At that point Jack Dunn, in need of ready cash, made a deal with the Red Sox. For a little over $8,000 he sold Boston Ruth, Ernie Shore, and catcher Ben Egan.

Harry Hooper remembered when Ruth reported to the team that July. "He had never been anywhere, didn't know anything about manners or how to behave among people—just a big overgrown green pea. You probably remember him with that big belly he got later on. But that wasn't there in 1914. George was six-foot-two and weighed one hundred ninety-eight pounds, all of it muscle. He had a slim waist, huge biceps, and no self-discipline, and not much education—not so very different from a lot of other nineteen-year-old would-be ballplayers. Except for two things: he could eat more than anyone else, and he could hit a baseball further."

Ruth remained with the Sox for a few weeks, then was sent down to Providence of the International League for more seasoning. He returned to the Red Sox at the end of the season for a little more work. Overall, the new man was 2–1 with an ERA of 3.91 for 23 innings of pitching.

After the 1914 season, Connie Mack broke up his team—winners of four of the last five pennants. Connie never gave a satisfactory reason as to why he did this. One theory is that his star players were asking for more money than he wanted to pay; another held that Mack was so disenchanted with the way his club lost the 1914 World Series to a decidedly inferior Boston Braves club in four straight that he acted out of pique. In any event, the following season saw Eddie Collins playing for Chicago, Jack Barry for Boston, Chief Bender and Eddie Plank jumped to the Federal League, and Herb Pennock also with the Red Sox.

With the A's out of contention, the pennant race was wide open and the vacuum was filled by the Red Sox and Tigers. On the strength of superior pitching, Boston managed to stay a few games ahead of the stronger-hitting Tigers, who featured the punishing bats of outfielders Ty Cobb, Sam Crawford, and Bobby Veach. When the race was over Boston stood at 101–50, and Detroit 100–54.

Carrigan's pitching was the best in the league. The ace in 1915 was Rube Foster with a 19–8 record, followed by Shore at 18–8, Ruth 18–8, Leonard 15–7, and sore-armed Joe Wood 15–5. Wood, pitching in excruciating pain whenever he took the mound, still flashed enough to post a league-leading 1.49 ERA. The club also had on the roster two youngsters earmarked for future greatness—twenty-three-year-old righty Carl Mays and twenty-one-year-old Pennock. Second baseman Jack Barry, for years one of the mainstays of Connie Mack's championship infields, was acquired in mid-season.

The pitching carried the club in 1915, with only Speaker among the regulars hitting over .300 (.322). The other .300 hitter on the squad was pitcher Ruth, batting .315 with four home runs. Babe's four long ones may not seem like much until one checks the records for 1915 and notes that the league leader, Braggo Roth, won the home run title with seven. Pitcher Ruth outhomered every one of his Red Sox teammates, none of whom hit more than two big-bangers. Needless to say, Boston fans were quick to take the big, good-natured, hard-hitting star pitcher to their hearts.

The 1915 World Series matched the Red Sox with the Philadelphia Phillies. The Phillies were not an outstanding team, but they did have one incomparable asset—right-hander

Grover Cleveland Alexander, a 31-game winner, and at the age of twenty-eight successor to Mathewson as the league's top pitcher.

Carrigan selected Shore to open the Series against Alexander in Philadelphia. Ernie pitched well, but a combination of infield bleeders and Alexander's fine pitching undid him and the Sox lost the opener, 3–1. The second game saw a bit of history unfold when Woodrow Wilson became the first president of the United States ever to attend a World Series game. With timing unbecoming a president or any other politico, Wilson caused a delay in the game by showing up twenty minutes late. When things finally got underway, Foster pitched the first of three consecutive 2–1 victories for Boston.

Games Three and Four were played in Boston, but not in Fenway Park. Because Braves Field, home of the Boston Braves, had a larger seating capacity than Fenway, the Red Sox players elected to play their home games in the National League park. (The enchantment of the Big Buck did not originate in the 1970s.) Leonard and Shore pitched the 2–1 wins in Boston and the Series returned to Philadelphia.

Rube Foster won the finale, struggling through to a 5–4 win. The Sox won this game in a highly uncharacteristic fashion—hitting home runs. Duffy Lewis, who had two homers all season long, parked one in the center field bleachers in the eighth inning to turn a 4–2 Boston deficit into a 4–4 tie. In the ninth inning Hooper, who also had hit just two four-baggers during the season, hit his second of the game. The shot provided the Red Sox with their 5–4 margin.

In 1914 and 1915 the National and American Leagues had been getting some nagging competition from a self-proclaimed third major league, a pretender that called itself the Federal League. This concoction was doomed to last just two years before falling apart. But before it went, it had an impact on the Red Sox.

Because it came bustling into existence with some handsomely bankrolled backers, the Federal League caused a bidding war similar to what had occurred when the American League proclaimed its major league status and began

wooing contracted players with the jingle of coin. In order to hold on to their stars, the National and American League club owners had to raise salaries, an action some of the owners looked upon as being nothing short of heretical and unpatriotic. But they had little choice. Among the big gainers was Tris Speaker, acknowledged as one of the game's two greatest players (Ty Cobb was the other). Tris was getting a salary of around $18,000 and Red Sox owner Joe Lannin didn't think that was at all funny.

So when the Federal League and its egregious temptations ceased to exist, Lannin moved to cut his star player's salary. The instrument he used was a meat cleaver: Joe told Tris he was cutting Speaker's salary in half. Tris told him where to stuff the whole thing. Like Grant at Vicksburg, each staked his position and prepared to fight it out if it took all summer long.

It seemed by spring training that some sort of agreement had been arrived at whereby Speaker would settle for a wage of $15,000, loose change today but royal bucks back then. Speaker wanted to remain in Boston, and perhaps he accepted Lannin's logic that he was deserving of having surgery done on his salary after seeing his batting average decrease for three straight years, from .383 to .365 to .338 to .322.

Suddenly there was a turnabout that stunned Red Sox fans: Lannin succumbed to a Cleveland bid of $50,000 for Speaker. The Red Sox also got infielder Fred Thomas, now little more than a footnote to their history, and right-hander Sam Jones, who turned out to be a pretty good pitcher.

Boston fans were outraged. They took deep and justified pride in having Speaker in their outfield, and now he was gone, and broken forever was the brilliant Lewis-Speaker-Hooper combine. (What Red Sox fans did not know was that the sale of Speaker would pale in comparison to what was just a few years down the road.)

In spite of the loss of their top player, Carrigan's men ran off a second straight pennant, thanks to some clutch September baseball. It was a three-way dogfight between Boston, Chicago, and Detroit. A highly successful September road trip by Boston during which they took two out of three from Chicago and three in a row from Detroit all but sealed the verdict.

Again it was primarily the pitching staff that did it. Young Babe Ruth, now all of twenty-one years old, emerged as the ace with a 23–12 record, with league-leading numbers in ERA (1.75) and shutouts (9). Leonard was 18–12 and Carl Mays, now a top starter, was 19–13. Shore was 15–10, Foster 14–7.

Without Speaker (who batted a ripe .386 for Cleveland), the offense struggled, with Larry Gardner's .308 heading up the hitters. The new center fielder, Clarence (Tilly) Walker, picked up from the Browns, batted .266. Along with their superior pitching, the Red Sox could also boast the league's finest defensive unit, leading with the highest fielding percentage and fewest errors. The inner defense of Hoblitzell, Barry, Scott, and Gardner was particularly sure-handed.

Boston's opponent in the 1916 World Series was the Brooklyn Dodgers. The Brooks had a solid team; their .261 club average led the National League and was 13 points better than Boston's. Their offense was led by first baseman Jake Daubert and outfielder Zack Wheat. Also on the squad was a wisecracking twenty-five-year-old outfielder named Casey Stengel. Even in those early years Stengel was the irrepressible spirit New York fans came to know decades later. Ernie Shore and Duffy Lewis encountered him on the field during batting practice before Game One.

"Hello, boys," Stengel said. "What do you think your losing share is going to come to?"

The supremely confident Sox players laughed at him. "We didn't think it was possible for anybody to beat us," Shore said. "Our pitching was too good."

Shore was right. With Ernie himself winning two games, the Red Sox took the Series in five games. It was their fourth World Series and fourth world championship. It was an unremarkable Series, except for Game Two.

The 14-inning second game of the 1916 World Series remains the longest by innings in Series history, as well as one of the fall classic's supreme pitching achievements. The job was turned in by baseball's premier left-hander, George Herman Ruth. The Babe started Game Two at Boston against Brooklyn southpaw Sherrod Smith. In the top of the first Brooklyn's Hy Myers came to bat with two out and nobody on and slashed a line drive into right-center that Tilly Walker ran down; but by the time the relay came in, Myers had an inside-the-park home run. In the Boston third Everett Scott tripled and scored on a ground ball by Ruth. After that, the door was shut until the bottom of the fourteenth, when Boston scored the winning run. Young Mr. Ruth had turned in 13⅓ consecutive scoreless innings, the first of many spectacular shows he was destined to put on in the World Series, although most of them were accomplished at home plate rather than on the mound.

After the Red Sox had won the championship by polishing off the Dodgers in Game Five, Manager Bill Carrigan moved about the clubhouse saying his farewells. The tough-minded, thirty-two-year-old player-manager had announced his retirement from baseball to enter the banking business in his hometown of Lewiston, Maine. Bill was leaving behind an almost spotless managerial record: three full seasons, one second-place finish, two pennants, and two world championships. Ruth, who later played for managerial giants Miller Huggins and Joe McCarthy, always maintained that Carrigan was the best manager he ever played under.

Carrigan's was not the only departure after the 1916 season. Owner Joseph Lannin had decided to sell out, despite the fact that the club was enjoying healthy financial success. Bothered by nagging ill health and weary of bickering with the autocratic Ban Johnson, who ran his league with the uncomplicated tyranny of a Mafia godfather, Lannin put the club up for sale and had no trouble finding a buyer. Nobody knew it at the time, but the deal was soon to become the worst disaster ever to befall Red Sox baseball. It was also destined to alter baseball history.

Above: Eddie Cicotte pitched for the Sox from 1908 to 1912. He was a 15-game winner in 1910. Traded to the White Sox in 1912, he went on to greatness and infamy.

Charley Hall, nicknamed "Sea Lion." He worked the mound in Boston from 1909 through 1913, with a 15–8 record in 1912 his best showing.

Patsy Donovan, manager of the Red Sox in 1910 and 1911.

Smoky Joe Wood in 1912, the year he won 34 games.

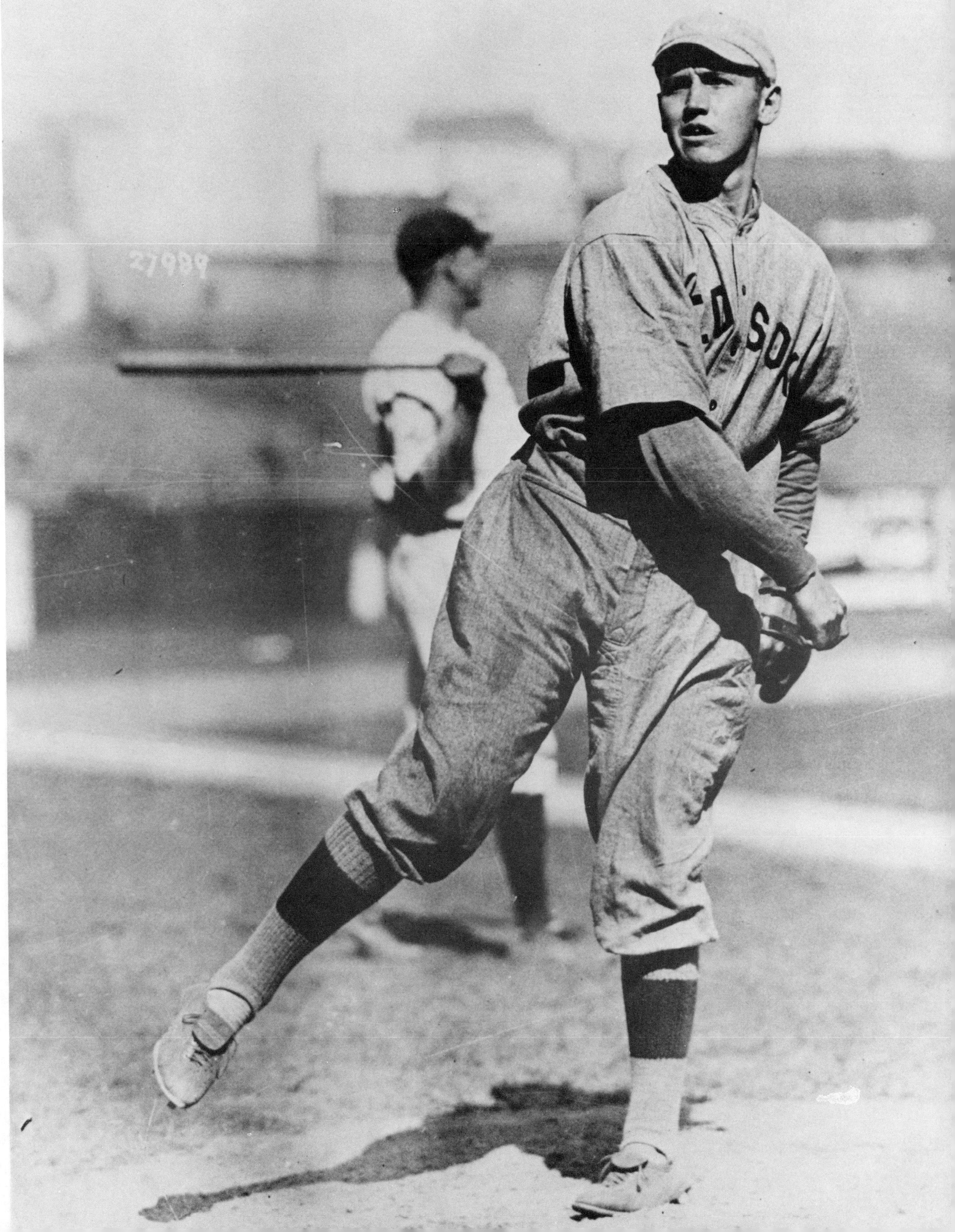

Left: Steve Yerkes, who gave the Red Sox some steady work at second and short from 1911 to 1914, when he jumped to the Federal League.

Below: Larry Gardner, one of the Red Sox' finest third basemen. He played with them from 1908 through 1917. His best year was 1912 when he batted .315.

Clyde Engle, the man who hit that famous fly ball to Fred Snodgrass in the last game of the 1912 World Series. Acquired from the Yankees in 1910, Clyde, who played both infield and outfield, remained with Boston until 1914, when he jumped to the Federal League.

28

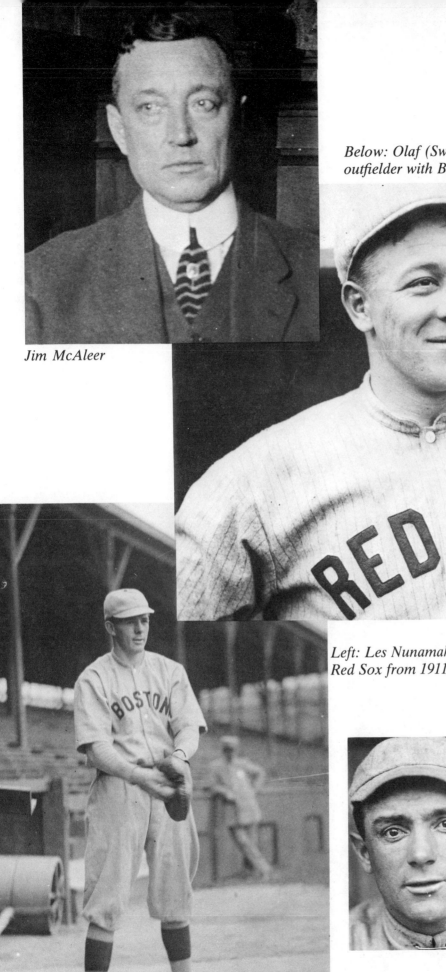

Jim McAleer

Below: Olaf (Swede) Henriksen, utility outfielder with Boston from 1911 to 1917.

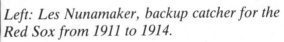

Left: Les Nunamaker, backup catcher for the Red Sox from 1911 to 1914.

Charles (Heinie) Wagner, one of the solid men of the Red Sox infield in the pre–World War I era. He later managed the club in 1930.

29

Catcher Forest (Hick) Cady was with the club from 1912 to 1917.

Tris Speaker

Ray Collins pitched for the Red Sox from 1909 to 1915. In 1913 and 1914 he was a two-time 20-game winner.

HARRIS & EWING
WASHINGTON, D.C.

Hugh Bedient's best year with the Red Sox was his rookie one in 1912 when he was 18–9. He jumped to the Federal League in 1915.

Buck O'Brien joined the Red Sox in 1911, won 19 games in 1912, and a year later was washed up with a sore arm.

Joe Wood (left) and Walter Johnson before their historic matchup in September 1912.

Joe Wood (left) and Tris Speaker on the front porch of their boarding house. They were roommates and inseparable friends.

*Wood and Mathewson pose during the 1912
World Series.*

*Hemmed in by the overflow crowd, Wood
warms up before his duel with Johnson. Straw
hats seem to be the order of the day.*

33

Bill Carrigan

Acquired from Cincinnati during the 1914 season, first baseman Dick Hoblitzell playe with the Red Sox until 1918.

Part of the victory parade after Boston won the 1912 Series. Standing up in front of the car is Mayor John F. "Honey Fitz" Fitzgerald, sitting in back are Jake Stahl, on the left, and Joe Wood.

Another member of Boston's superb pitching staff of the era, right-hander George (Rube) Foster. He worked for the Sox from 1913 through 1917, when he retired. His top year was 1915 when he was 19–8.

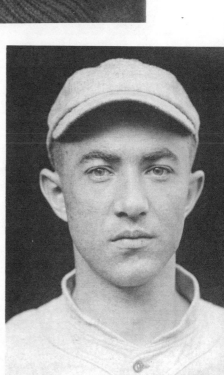

Dutch Leonard pitched brilliantly for the Red Sox from 1913 to 1918. He was 18–5 in 1914 with baseball's lowest earned run average ever, 1.01.

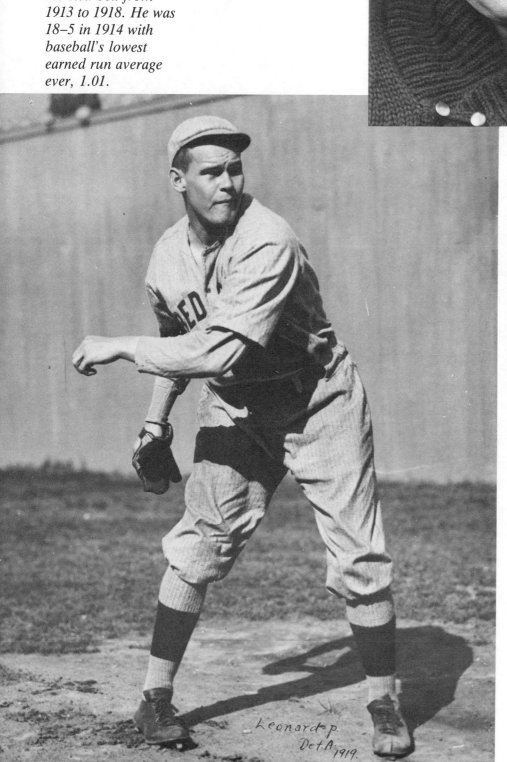

Everett Scott, Boston's fine-fielding shortstop from 1914 through 1921, when he became part of the exodus to New York.

35

Chester (Pinch) Thomas, reserve catcher from
1912 through 1917.

Harry Hooper. Harry was traded to the White
Sox in 1921 for outfielders Shano Collins and
Nemo Leibold.

*A three-time 20-game winner with Cleveland,
southpaw Vean Gregg was acquired by Boston
in 1914. He pitched for the Red Sox through
1916 but never regained his earlier brilliance.*

*Del Gainor. Del was obtained from Detroit
early in the 1914 season and stayed with Boston
until 1919, mostly as a backup first baseman.*

Ernie Shore, one of Boston's aces from 1914 to 1917. In 1915 he was 18–8, his best year.

Hal Janvrin, utility infielder for the Red Sox from 1911 to 1917.

37

Babe Ruth

Tris Speaker, traded to Cleveland in the spring of 1916.

Speaker's replacement in center field, Clarence (Tilly) Walker, acquired from the Browns. Tilly put in two years and then moved on to Philadelphia.

Picked up from the Athletics in 1915, Jack Barry played second base for the Red Sox until 1919. He managed the club in 1917.

Jack Dunn, owner of the Baltimore Orioles. The man who sold Babe Ruth to the Red Sox.

Starting pitchers for Game One of the 1915 World Series: Boston's Ernie Shore (left) and Philadelphia's Grover Cleveland Alexander.

Action in the 1915 Series. It's the first inning of Game Two. Tris Speaker is being called out at second on an attempted steal. Applying the tag is second baseman Bert Niehoff. Tris was the back end of a double steal; the front man, Harry Hooper, made home on the play.

That's Tilly Walker sliding into third on his triple in the first inning of the first game of the 1916 World Series, at Fenway. The third baseman is Mike Mowrey. The hustling umpire is none other than former Red Sox pitcher Bill Dinneen.

40

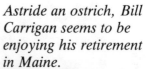

Rival managers Wilbert Robinson (left) and Bill Carrigan doing the traditional thing before the start of the 1916 World Series between Brooklyn and Boston.

Astride an ostrich, Bill Carrigan seems to be enjoying his retirement in Maine.

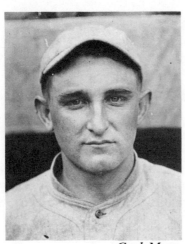

Carl Mays

That's skipper Bill Carrigan at bat in Game Four of the 1916 Series, played at Ebbets Field in Brooklyn. The catcher is Chief Meyers, the umpire John Quigley.

Drawing a crowd at home plate is Larry Gardner, who is sliding in safely on an inside-the-park home run. It was a 3-run shot, in the second inning of Game Four in Brooklyn. The man leaning forward behind the plate is Dick Hoblitzell, who scored on the blow. The player with the bats is on-deck hitter Everett Scott. The catcher is Chief Meyers, the umpire John Quigley.

3 · RAPE

THE NEW OWNER WAS HARRY FRAZEE, a thirty-six-year-old native of Peoria, Illinois. This product of the Midwest was brimming with ambition and had stars in his eyes—only they weren't baseball stars. Harry's compelling desire was to produce plays on Broadway: musical comedies in particular. The Broadway virus has been known to cloud the thinking and impair the judgment of many an otherwise rational person, and few people suffered the ill effects as severely as Harry Frazee. If his purpose had simply been to make money, he could have sat back and slid his fingers through the profits his ball club was turning. Also, his showman's instincts would have been appeased knowing that he owned the contract of what was soon to become The Greatest Show on Earth, with performances every afternoon from April through September and sometimes extended into October. The name of this show was George Herman Ruth and on any given day he might be outdrawing the combined attendances of every theater in town.

But Harry Frazee wanted to make it big on Broadway. And thus was the termite set loose in the Red Sox structure.

With second baseman Jack Barry managing, the club finished second in 1917, 9 games behind a Chicago White Sox club that in the next three years would take two pennants and throw one World Series. Again it was pitching that kept the team afloat. Ruth, carving out his superman image with the loudest hammer and keenest chisel in the land, was 24–13 with 6 shutouts, 2.01 ERA, and 35 complete games in 38 starts. In addition he batted .325 and hit 2 of the team's 14 home runs. Combining his diamond feats with a big, outgoing, ingenuous personality, he was rapidly becoming the most popular man in Boston.

Following Babe on the mound was Carl Mays with a 22–9 record, Dutch Leonard 16–17, and Ernie Shore 13–10.

On June 23 that summer Ruth and Shore lent their names to one of baseball's memorable games. Ruth was the starting pitcher on that warm, memory-book afternoon at Fenway. Boston was playing Washington. The first batter to face Ruth was second baseman Ray Morgan, about to become one of baseball's sterling trivia names. Ruth walked Morgan and immediately began jawing at umpire Brick Owens. After a few exchanges, Babe blew his stack and threatened to rearrange Owens's smile, whereupon the umpire thumbed him from the premises.

This presented skipper Jack Barry with a problem: a ball game was underway and he had no pitcher. So he turned to Shore and said, "Go in there and stall around until I can get somebody warmed up." Barry had no intention of leaving Shore in the game. But Ernie began pitching. On his first delivery, Morgan was thrown out stealing. Shore retired the next two men easily. Barry decided to leave him in.

"I don't believe I threw seventy-five pitches that whole game," Shore recalled. "They just kept hitting it right at somebody. They didn't hit but one ball hard and that was in the ninth inning. John Henry, the catcher, lined one on the nose, but right at Duffy Lewis in left field. That was the second out in the ninth. Then Clark Griffith, who was managing Washington, sent a fellow named Mike Menosky in to bat for the pitcher. Griffith was a hard loser, a very hard loser. He didn't want to see me complete that perfect game. So he had Menosky drag a bunt, just to try and break it up. Menosky could run, too. He was fast. He dragged a good bunt past me, but Jack Barry came in and made just a wonderful one-hand stab of the ball, scooped it up and got him at first. That was a good, sharp ending to the game, which I won by a score of four to zero."

After some deliberation by the league, it was decided to credit Shore with a perfect game, and so it went into the record books. It remains one of six perfect games in American League history, with two of them spun out by Red Sox pitchers, Cy Young having done it earlier.

The 1918 season was to prove Boston's last full feast for a long, long time. The team won its fourth pennant and fourth World Series in seven years. So no one ever dreamed it possible that the next time the Sox finished in the first division would be 1934. But that is exactly the destiny that was beginning to darken the Red Sox horizon.

Because of the war, now raging in its full, terrible splendor in Europe, the baseball season ended on September 2. The Provost Marshall had issued a "work-or-fight" order, which bluntly meant all draft-age men had to join the military or get into an essential industry. Baseball was ruled nonessential (how little the government understood the priorities of Red Sox fans), though it did receive dispensation to play until September 2 before facing the full blast of the draft.

But even with the dispensation, the Red Sox were particularly hard hit. Some of their finest players, beginning with Manager Jack Barry, marched off to make the world safe for democracy, including Duffy Lewis, infielder Hal Janvrin, and pitchers Ernie Shore, Herb Pennock, and Dutch Leonard.

At that time Frazee was still well heeled and he opened his wallet to acquire some excellent players from Connie Mack, who needed the cash. Included in the transactions were first baseman Stuffy McInnis, catcher Wally Schang, outfielder Amos Strunk, and right-hander Bullet Joe Bush, each of whom contributed handsomely to that wartime pennant.

Outhit by six of the seven other clubs in the league, the Sox once again did it with pitching. Mays was 21–13, Bush 15–15, Sam Jones 16–5, and Ruth 13–7. The Babe started only

19 games; he was spending more and more time in the outfield now, as well as putting in some time at first base after McInnis swapped his bat for a rifle. All told, he got into 95 games, batted an even .300, and won the first of his many home run titles with 11 (the club overall hit 15). It still may not seem like a lot, but it was more than the team totals of Cleveland, Washington, St. Louis, and Chicago. The young man's pitching days were clearly behind him now. The man who found the thunder in Ruth's bat too hard to resist was the club's new skipper, Ed Barrow, who would later help mastermind the Yankee dynasty as the club's general manager.

The Babe had one last burst of pitching glory in the 1918 World Series, won by Boston over the Chicago Cubs four games to two. Pitching the opener against Chicago's own superb southpaw, Jim (Hippo) Vaughan, Ruth spun a fine 6-hit shutout and thus extended his World Series string of goose eggs, dating back to 1916, to 22⅓ innings, 5⅓ frames under Christy Mathewson's record. He came back in Game Four and hurled another 7⅓ blankers before finally being scored upon. It gave him a grand total of 29⅔ consecutive scoreless World Series innings, which held as a record until broken by Whitey Ford in 1961. The double-threat that was Babe Ruth was in full evidence in that game. In the bottom of the fourth Ruth tripled in 2 runs, a crucial blow in the 3–2 Red Sox victory.

Two days later, on September 11, Carl Mays hurled his second victory of the Series, giving the Red Sox the championship, and making them five-for-five in World Series play.

The future looked bright for the Boston Red Sox. They had taken three pennants and three championships in four years. Their pitching was deep, talented, and young, even with Ruth making the move from the mound to the outfield. Mays was a 20-game winner, Sam Jones and Joe Bush were winners, and coming along were two brilliant starters named Herb Pennock and Waite Hoyt. Wally Schang was a good catcher with a .300 bat, Stuffy McInnis at first base was one of the best, as was Everett Scott at short, and Harry Hooper was still performing his miracles in right field.

But above all was Ruth, about to explode to greatness in 1919. The game had never seen, nor has it since, a 20-game winner who could also lead the league in home runs; a youngster whose talent was made all the more magnetic by an exuberant, oversized personality that charmed and enchanted fans everywhere.

But the storm clouds were gathering. In New York, Colonel Jacob Ruppert, who had bought the Yankees a few years earlier, was determined to make his club a winner, and backing this desire was an ability and a willingness to spend. In contrast, Harry Frazee was beginning to run into cash flow problems. With theatrical investment still his dominant passion and obsession, Harry was continuing to back Broadway shows, and through the alchemy of poor judgment and critical displeasure, these shows were turning into big, expensive turkeys. With every negative review from the typewriters of the Broadway critics, the disintegration of the Boston Red Sox was becoming more inevitable.

It began quietly enough after the 1918 season with the sale of service returnees Duffy Lewis and Ernie Shore to the Yankees. The transaction was of little import, since Lewis was at the end of the string and Shore had come up with a bad arm. But it was an ominous beginning.

Midway through the 1919 season Carl Mays walked off the mound in the middle of a game in disgust with what he deemed some shoddy play behind him. The talented but temperamental pitcher announced he would never again pitch for the Red Sox. Shortly after, he was dispatched to the Yankees for two pitchers and $40,000. The deal outraged Ban Johnson, who had sought to suspend Mays for his action. But the autocrat of the American League ran smack into the tough-minded Jacob Ruppert. The colonel brought an injunction to restrain Johnson and after some storming about the courtrooms, Ban backed down and Mays joined the Yankees. It was the beginning of an erosion of Johnson's authority and helped pave the way for the appointment of Judge Kenesaw Mountain Landis as the game's commissioner and supreme authority in November 1920.

The Sox tumbled to a tie for fifth place in 1919 despite a fine 16–8 showing from Pennock. Nevertheless it was an exciting season for Red Sox fans, thanks to the maturing, explosive bat of Ruth. Almost exclusively an outfielder now (he started just 15 games and had an 8–5 record), the Babe ripped into his specialty and turned in a record-shattering performance by hitting an unheard-of 29 home runs. He didn't just break the record; he left it in shambles. In 1902 Ralph (Socks) Seybold had poled 16 homers for the Athletics, setting the American League standard. Buck Freeman's 13 a year later was as close as anyone had since come. And Ruth wasn't just hitting them— he was putting them out of sight. To deadball–era fans, used to the offensive standard being Ty Cobb's well-placed line drives and skillful drag bunts, Ruth was like a creature from another planet. As one indicator of the man's dominance, one need only note that in 1919 the Red Sox hit 33 home runs—29 of them by Babe Ruth.

The boom was lowered on Boston on January 6, 1920. Four years after the sale of Tris Speaker to Cleveland, Red Sox fans suffered an even greater indignity—the sale of Babe Ruth to the Yankees. Compounding the insult was the fact that it was a straight cash deal— $125,000. No players in return, just a pile of money to help Harry Frazee out of debt. But not even that considerable sum of money was enough. Frazee was so far behind his creditors (or so far ahead of them, depending on economic perspective), that Ruppert took a $350,000 mortgage on Fenway Park.

Not since the Battle of Bunker Hill did an event so thoroughly shake Boston. The loss of Ruth not only wrecked Red Sox baseball for decades, it also provided the cornerstone upon which the Yankees went on to build the most stunning dynasty in all sports history, a dynasty that continued to flatten the Red Sox decades later when the Sox finally became healthy again.

The Ruth sale, baseball's all-time blockbuster transaction, was only the beginning. Conveniently for the debt-ridden Frazee and the monied Ruppert, Harry's theatrical office was practically next door to Jake's Yankee office on New York's 42nd Street. Whenever

Harry needed some ready cash, all he had to do was take a short stroll and drop in on Jake. Andwith his Broadway shows hitting the New York stages like so much wet lettuce, Harry took the walk often.

It has gone down in baseball annals as "The Rape of the Red Sox." And while it was going on, the game's newly appointed czar, Judge Landis, invested with dictatorial powers and charged with upholding the game's integrity, looked the other way. Why Landis ignored the systematic destruction of a baseball team has never been satisfactorily explained. A possible explanation is that he was unwilling to tangle with the iron-willed Ruppert. The colonel had, after all, forced the formidable Ban Johnson to back down.

Over the next few years the following Red Sox players were dealt to New York: pitchers Waite Hoyt, Joe Bush, Sam Jones, George Pipgras, and Herb Pennock; shortstop Everett Scott, third baseman Joe Dugan, catcher Wally Schang. When the Yankees took their first pennant in 1921, ex-Red Sox pitchers won 48 games for them; in 1922, when the Yankees won another pennant, ex-Red Sox pitchers won 70 games for them; and in 1923, when the Yankees took a third straight pennant, the Boston-bred contingent won 82 games. As late as 1928, a Yankee pennant-winner still had ex-Red Sox pitchers winning 64 games for the club.

What hurt most, of course, was the loss of Ruth. Not only were the Yankees winning pennants by the fistful, but sullen Red Sox fans had to sit by and watch their old favorite rewrite the record book with the most colossal slugging feats ever seen in the game's history, before or since. Years later Ernie Shore would sum it up ruefully: "When they talk about a Yankee dynasty, I say it was really a Red Sox dynasty, in a Yankee uniform."

And so began a wandering in the wilderness exceeded only by that of Moses and the Israelites.' In 1920 and 1921 the club still had enough left to finish fifth. From 1922 through 1930 they wound up dead last, with the exception of 1924, when they beat out Chicago by a half-game for seventh.

In 1923 Harry Frazee sold the club. The in-evitable came too late. The new owner was Bob Quinn, a good baseball man, but handicapped by lack of funds. It was not a sinking ship that Quinn bought, but rather a sunk one, broadsided by the torpedos of U-Boat Harry Frazee. Predictably, and understandably, Bostonians stayed away from Fenway in droves through the miserable decade of the 1920s. Ironically, the few large crowds that turned out came to stare wistfully when Ruth led the Yankees into town.

There was more irony in 1925 when Harry Frazee struck producer's gold on Broadway with a classy musical called *No, No, Nanette*, which earned him tons of money. There was a final, personal irony for Harry A few years after finally achieving his goal of Broadway success, Frazee died at the age of forty-eight. And although *No, No, Nanette* remains in the theatrical repertory as a frequently revived hit show, Harry Frazee will forever be remembered as The Man Who Sold Babe Ruth.

The Red Sox bumbled on through the 1920s, a lost, predefeated team. Managers came and went. Ed Barrow left in 1920 to become general manager of the Yankees (no Boston talent, it seemed, was safe from the Yankee magnet). Barrow was followed by Hugh Duffy, a former outfielder for the Boston Nationals who in 1894 had batted .438, still the highest figure in all the annals of baseball. After Duffy came the old Chicago Cub hero Frank Chance. Frank was followed by Lee Fohl, who had had first division finishes with Cleveland and St. Louis for six consecutive years but who saw little daylight in Boston. In 1928 the old hero Bill Carrigan was coaxed out of retirement, but the former World Series victor spent three years in the cobwebs of last place. Bill was followed by former Red Sox shortstop Heinie Wagner, Shano Collins, Marty McManus, and Bucky Harris, who in 1934 lifted the club into the heady atmosphere of fourth place, in those days high enough to give Red Sox fans a nose bleed. Nine managers in fifteen years.

Along the way some fairly good ballplayers came and went. First baseman George Burns batted .328 in 1923 and was rewarded by being traded to Cleveland. Right-hander Howard Ehmke won 20 games in 1923 and 19 the next year. In 1927 the Red Sox made a steal of a deal with Washington, acquiring young second baseman Buddy Myer. Buddy batted .313 in 1928 and was promptly traded back to Washington where he became a perennial .300 hitter and a batting champion in 1935.

In May 1930 Red Sox fans had a case of déjà vu. The club had a big, strong, hard-throwing right-hander named Charlie (Red) Ruffing. After joining the club in 1925, Ruffing had had year after year of losing seasons, but so did the Red Sox. In May 1930, in need of money, Bob Quinn offered the Yankees the pick of one of three pitchers: Danny MacFayden, Ed Morris, or Ruffing. Both MacFayden and Morris had better records than Ruffing, but the canny Yankees chose Charlie. So, for $50,000 and

outfielder Cedric Durst, the Yankees once again skinned the Bosox in a deal, as Ruffing became one of the league's top pitchers for the next dozen years.

In 1932 the Red Sox suffered through the most dismal year in their history, winning 43 and losing 111. Attendance shrank to 182,000, or around 2,400 per game.

The disastrous 1932 season marked the end of the line for owner Bob Quinn. Broke, debt-ridden, Quinn had no choice but to put the club on the market. In late February 1933 a deal had been agreed upon. For an estimated million dollars the Red Sox had been sold to a thirty-year-old millionaire named Thomas Austin Yawkey.

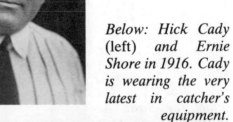

Ed Barrow

Below: Hick Cady (left) and Ernie Shore in 1916. Cady is wearing the very latest in catcher's equipment.

Babe Ruth

John (Stuffy) McInnis. Stuffy joined the Red Sox in 1918, hit .300 a couple of times, and was dealt to Cleveland in 1922. In 1921 he played 152 games at first base for Boston and made just one error for a .999 fielding average.

Bullet Joe Bush. Acquired from the A's in 1918, Joe threw his bullets for the Red Sox until 1921. He was 16–9 in 1920, good enough to get him traded to the Yankees.

Amos Strunk roamed the Red Sox outfield in 1918 and part of 1919 before being traded back to Philadelphia, from whence he had come.

48

Fenway Park from the outside.

Catcher Wally Schang, traded by the A's to the Red Sox in 1918. Wally batted .306 and .305 in 1919 and 1920 and then took the train to New York.

Herb Pennock, greatest of the Red Sox pitchers sent to New York. He was with Boston from 1916 through 1922. He returned in 1934 at the age of forty, posted a 2–0 record, and then retired. He graced American League mounds for twenty-two years and won 240 games, 61 of them for the Red Sox.

49

Sam Jones, pitcher. Acquired from Cleveland in the Speaker deal, Sam developed into a fine pitcher for Boston. He was 23–16 in 1921, which in those days was the same as a ticket to New York. Sam didn't retire until 1935, after pitching 22 years with six American League clubs and winning 229 games.

Al (Roxy) Walters, reserve catcher for the Red Sox from 1919 to 1921.

John (Shano) Collins. Shano came to Boston from the White Sox in the deal for Harry Hooper. He played for Boston from 1921 to 1925. He managed the team in 1931 and part of 1932.

Waite Hoyt, known as "Schoolboy." Hoyt joined Boston as an eighteen-year-old in 1919. In 1920 he was just 6–6, but the Yankees knew a good thing and got him in a trade the next year. Waite stayed on the job until 1938, pitching for seven teams in both leagues and retiring with 237 wins.

The Red Sox did a smart thing when they got third baseman Joe Dugan from the A's in 1922, then did a foolish one when they swapped him to the Yankees in the middle of the season.

Oscar Vitt, Red Sox infielder from 1919 to 1923.

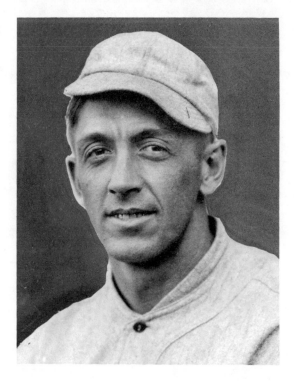

Above: First baseman-outfielder Joe Harris joined the Red Sox in 1922, batted .316, .335, and .303 before being traded to Washington.

Above: The Red Sox got outfielder Ira Flagstead from Detroit in 1923 and Ira gave them six solid seasons before being swapped to Washington in 1929. His top year was .311 in 1923.

Right: Right-hander Ray Caldwell was one who went from New York to Boston in 1919. He worked a few months for the Red Sox who then shipped him to Cleveland, where he won 20 games the next season.

Far left: The Red Sox acquired Washington's long-time third baseman Eddie Foster in 1920. He was traded to the Browns in 1922.

Near left: First baseman George Burns, obtained from Cleveland in 1922 as part of the Stuffy McInnis deal. George played two years for the Red Sox, batted .306 and .328, and was traded back to Cleveland.

52

Near right: Harry Frazee

Far right: Hugh Duffy, Red Sox skipper in 1921 and 1922.

It's June 27, 1922, and Red Sox infielder Pinky Pittenger has just stolen home against the Yankees on the front end of a double steal. The catcher is ex-Red Soxer Wally Schang.

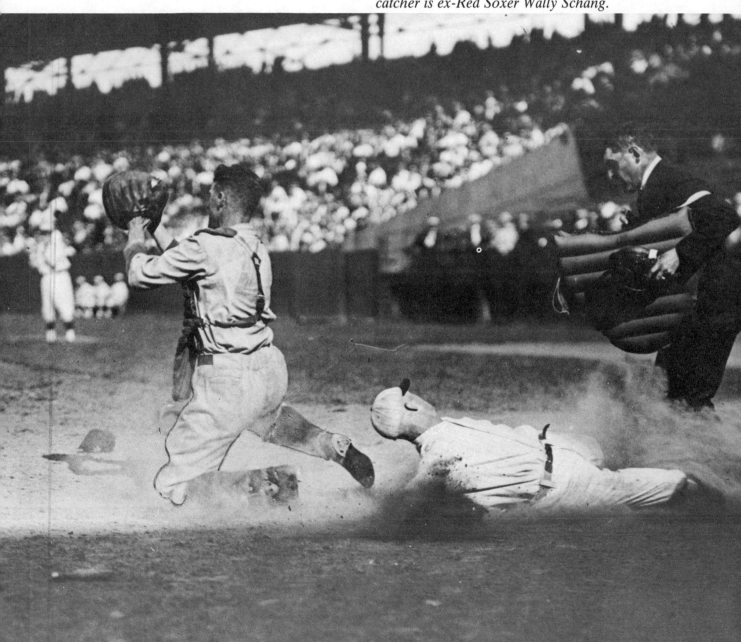

The Red Sox got a good one when they acquired catcher Herold (Muddy) Ruel from the Yankees in 1921, but they couldn't stand the prosperity and traded him to Washington two years later.

The Red Sox were the guests when Yankee Stadium opened in 1923. From left to right, Yankee manager Miller Huggins, Yankee owner Jacob Ruppert, and brand-new Red Sox manager Frank Chance.

Outfielder Ike Boone, who swung a mean bat for the Red Sox in 1924 and 1925, batting .333 and .330, his only full years with the team. He never repeated that success anywhere else.

Right-hander Jack Russell, a good pitcher who labored for some awful Red Sox teams from 1926 to 1932.

Below: Boston got a top-flight pitcher when they got right-hander Howard Ehmke from the Tigers in 1923. Ehmke was 20–17 that year, 19–17 the next. He was traded to the A's in 1926.

Above: Right-hander Alex Ferguson pitched for the Red Sox from 1922 to 1925. In 1924 he was 14–17, his best year. He was traded to Washington in 1925.

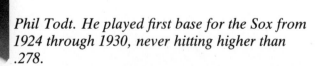

Phil Todt. He played first base for the Sox from 1924 through 1930, never hitting higher than .278.

Bill Regan, Boston second baseman from 1926 through 1930. Bill's best year was 1929 when he batted .288.

Red Sox third baseman in 1926 and part of '27, Fred Haney. Thirty years later he won a couple of pennants managing the Milwaukee Braves.

57

It's 1927 and Bill Carrigan is back at the helm. Bill, shown here with Miller Huggins, knew the good old days were gone forever when he suffered through three last-place finishes.

Near right: Infielder Buddy Myer was obtained from Washington in 1927, batted .288 and .313 for the Sox, and was then traded back to Washington in 1929. It was one of Boston's worst deals ever, which is saying something.

Far right: After a great slugging career with the Browns, Bill (Baby Doll) Jacobson joined the Red Sox in 1926. He batted .305, then was released the following year.

Johnny Tobin, another former star in the Browns outfield, played with Boston in 1926 and 1927. In '27 he batted .310, then was released.

Below: The Red Sox obtained Bill (Slim) Harriss from the A's in 1926. He led the staff with 14 wins in 1927. He was released a year later.

Above: Red Sox manager Lee Fohl and Yankee Skipper Miller Huggins in 1926.

John Heving, backup catcher for the Red Sox during the 1920s.

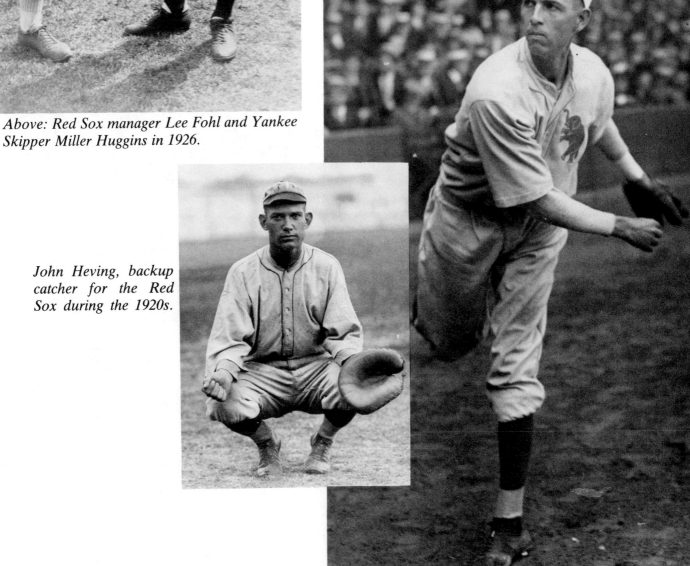

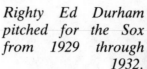

Righty Ed Durham pitched for the Sox from 1929 through 1932.

Danny MacFayden pitched for the Red Sox from 1926 to 1932. His best year was 1931 when he was 16–12.

Ed Morris, one of the club's better pitchers in the late 1920s. Ed won 19 in 1928, 14 the next year. He died in 1932, killed in a brawl.

Earl Webb, shown here in a Chicago Cubs uniform, played with the Red Sox from 1930 to midway through the 1932 season—not very long, but long enough to set a very enduring record. In 1931 Earl, an outfielder, established the all-time record for doubles in a season with 67. He batted .333 that year.

Roy Johnson, Red Sox outfielder from 1932 to 1935. From 1933 through 1935 his batting averages were .313, .320, .315.

60

Ken Williams, the third member of the St. Louis Browns' great outfield of the early 1920s to play with the Red Sox. Like Johnny Tobin and Baby Doll Jacobson, Ken's best years were behind him when he joined Boston. He still had enough hits in his bat, however, to bat .303 in 1928 and .345 as a part-timer the next year.

Red Ruffing

Far left: Smead Jolley could hit; his problem was fielding. Smead was in the outfield for Boston in 1932 and 1933, batting .312 and .282. His adventures with fly balls became so precarious, however, that he was soon back in the minors, where his prodigious hitting became legendary.

Near left: Allen (Dusty) Cooke, switch-hitting outfielder with the Sox from 1933 through 1936. Dusty's best was a .306 average in 1935.

Marty McManus, shown here with the Browns, played third for the Red Sox from 1931 to 1933, managing the club the last two years.

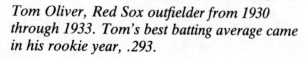

Tom Oliver, Red Sox outfielder from 1930 through 1933. Tom's best batting average came in his rookie year, .293.

Above: Dale Alexander, shown here with Detroit just before being traded to Boston early in the 1932 season, the year he went on to hit .367 and win the batting championship. The next year, however, he dropped to .281 and was released. A first baseman, the big guy was never considered a model of defensive propriety.

62

4 · RAYS OF SUNSHINE

IN TIME HE WAS TO BECOME as much a New England institution as Fenway Park and his beloved Red Sox. He was quiet, reserved, uncomplaining; toward his players he was generous and sentimental. He was the epitome of what the owner of a big league ball club should be. He spent lavishly to restore the former eminence of his team. And he was a fan, with enough boy in him to keep the lights on in Fenway after a night game and stand at home plate taking shots at his left field wall.

Yawkey came to baseball and money naturally. He was the nephew and later adopted son of Bill Yawkey, who once owned the Detroit Tigers and who left young Tom several million dollars in his will. Tom also inherited many more millions from his grandfather, who had holdings in lumber and ore. A product of Yale, where he had played a bit of second base, Yawkey took over the Red Sox with a minimum of fuss and a minimum of words. In his few words, however, was delivered his credo: "I don't intend to mess with a loser." His checkbook would be at the ready to help the team, he said, a statement that perked the ears of some of his financially pinched fellow owners in that Depression-ridden time.

Yawkey's first official act was to hire as his vice-president and general manager one of baseball's all-time players and one of its finest intellects, Eddie Collins. After more than two decades as the game's premier second baseman, Collins had been working for the Athletics as Connie Mack's top lieutenant.

The first of the many significant moves Yawkey was to make came in December 1933. For $125,000 and two second-line players, Boston acquired from the Athletics left-handed pitchers Lefty Grove and Rube Walberg and second baseman Max Bishop. Neither Walberg nor Bishop contributed much to the Red Sox' cause, but in Grove the club was getting the man who had been the league's dominant pitcher for years. For the previous seven years in succession, the fastballing Grove had won 20 or more games, including a 31–4 season in 1931.

The thirty-three-year-old Robert Moses Grove was not only the game's greatest pitcher, he was also one of its more vivid personalities. Dour, tempestuous, grimly competitive, Lefty was a hard loser, probably because he was not accustomed to it (his record during those previous seven years was 172–53). Once when he lost a tough one to the White Sox, Lefty came roaring into the clubhouse, shouting, "You think Grove is going to pitch his arm off for you hitless wonders?" So furious and indignant was he, Lefty refused to ride in the team bus with his mates, preferring the five-mile walk from Comiskey Park back to the hotel.

The Great Grove did not pay immediate dividends, however. He came up with a sore arm in spring training that held him to a mediocre 8–8 record in 1934. So embarrassed was Connie Mack at the thought that he might have palmed off damaged goods on Yawkey, he offered to refund Yawkey's money and reclaim Grove. An appreciative Yawkey declined with thanks.

If Grove was the most temperamental pitcher in the league, then the second was Cleveland right-hander Wes Ferrell, who had been known to smash his own wristwatch, chew on his own glove, and punch his own fist into his own jaw when the gods played mischief with him. In May 1934 the Red Sox added this handsome blond Vesuvius from the

Indians along with outfielder Dick Porter for a few players and 25,000 of Yawkey's bucks. (Ferrell's good looks were ruggedly classic. When Hollywood offered him a screen test Ferrell turned them down, saying, "I already have a job.")

Like Grove, Ferrell had left his good fastball somewhere on the trail and reported to the Sox in the new persona of a crafty control pitcher. A four-time 20-game winner with the Indians, Wes renewed the good habit in Boston by winning 25 in 1935 and 20 in 1936.

Ferrell won a lot of his own games with his hitting—he still holds the American League home run–hitting records for pitchers for a season (9) and career (36). One of Ferrell's cherished memories was of the time he pinch-hit a home run to win a game for the man he idolized beyond all others—Lefty Grove. Lefty, sure his well-pitched game was lost, had gone morosely to the clubhouse before Ferrell unloaded.

"So we all rush into the clubhouse," Wes remembered, "laughing and hollering, the way you do after a game like that. And here's Lefty, sitting there, still thinking he's lost his game. When he saw all the carrying-on, I tell you, the smoke started coming out of his ears.

"'I don't see what's so funny,' he says. 'A man loses a ball game and you're all carrying on.'

"Then somebody says, 'Hell, Lefty, we won it. Wes hit a home run for you.'

"Well, I was sitting across the clubhouse from him, pulling my uniform off and I notice he's staring at me, with just a trace of smile at the corners of his mouth. Just staring at me. He doesn't say anything. I give him a big grin and pull my sweat shirt up over my head. Then I hear him say, 'Hey, Wes.' I look over and he's rolling a bottle of wine across to me—he'd keep a bottle of one thing or another stashed up in his locker. So here it comes, rolling and bumping along the clubhouse floor. I picked it up and thanked him and put it in my locker. At the end of the season I brought it back to Carolina with me and let it sit up on the mantel. It sat up there for years and years. Every time I looked at it I thought of Old Left. He rolled it over to me."

The Yawkey era had begun with an almost complete housecleaning. Of the players who started the 1932 season, only one, pitcher Johnny Welch, remained as the 1934 season got underway. The new men were loose and eager, filled with the spirit of ballplayers who sense the elevator is going up. And there were practical jokes. Billy Werber remembered one that was pulled on Wes Ferrell.

"One spring in Sarasota Ferrell rented a car. Well, the car was sitting outside of the hotel one afternoon. Some of the guys went around to the back of the hotel where the garbage was put out and got a pile of crab guts and fish heads. Then they went to the car and lifted out the seat and dropped this filthy, foul-smelling stuff in there and replaced the seat. And of course that car stayed out there in a broiling Florida sun, all that day and the next day too.

"The following night Roy Johnson had a date and asked Wes if he could use the car. Wes, always the good fellow, said sure. When Roy opened the door the stench almost blew him over. There were some old clothes lying in the back that Wes used to wear when he fished, and Roy thought they were the cause of it. So he got rid of them and went along. He drove past the hotel later that evening with his date and she had her head stuck out the window on one side of the car and Roy had his head stuck out the window on the other side. When we asked him about it the next day, he said, 'It was the most horrible experience I've ever had. She thought it was me and I thought it was her.'"

Right after the 1934 season, Yawkey moved again. It was said that Washington Senators owner Clark Griffith would sell his own mother, if the price was right. Well, that deal never presented itself, but Griff came reasonably close—he sold his son-in-law to Yawkey for $250,000. No doubt many a father has dreamed of being able to peddle his daughter's husband, but in this case Griff was genuinely fond of Joe Cronin. In 1934, however, few men would have had the fiber to resist the lure of a quarter of a million.

Cronin was the twenty-eight-year-old short-stop-manager of the Senators, a handsome, lantern-jawed, San Francisco Irishman whose leadership and heavy hitting had led the Senators to an unexpected pennant in 1933. Swinging the meanest bat of any shortstop in the league, Joe was a .300 hitter who had driven in over 100 runs in each of the previous five seasons.

The Red Sox hit well for Cronin in Joe's first year—.276—but the bugaboo that was to haunt Red Sox teams for decade after decade was already in evidence—inadequate pitching. Ferrell won 25, Grove rebounded from his sore arm to win 20, but the rest of the staff might as well have stayed in bed. Still, the club finished fourth in an extremely tough, hard-hitting league that was headed by Detroit and New York, with the Yankees set to add Joe DiMaggio the next year and begin machine-gunning pennants with demoralizing regularity.

One of Boston's losses in 1935 was a memorable affair. It involved an instance of a player using his head as well as any ballplayer ever has. The Sox were playing Cleveland at Fenway on September 7. Going into the last of the ninth trailing 5–1, they launched a rally that scored 2 runs and had the bases loaded with none out. Cronin was at bat, facing Cleveland's Oral Hildebrand.

Joe came through with a ringing line drive right at third baseman Odell Hale. Hale could not get his glove up in time and the ball clobbered him square on the forehead. The ball caromed through the air to shortstop Bill Knickerbocker who flipped it to second baseman Roy Hughes who stepped on second to double up Billy Werber and then fired to first baseman Hal Trosky who tripled up the baserunner there. The stunned, embarrassed Odell Hale was then congratulated by his teammates for having started a triple play.

Mesmerized by his left field wall, Yawkey continued to seek out hitters to beef up his lineup. In December 1935 he shook another $150,000 out of his wallet and obtained from the Athletics first baseman Jimmie Foxx and pitcher Johnny Marcum. Marcum had won 17 for the last-place A's in 1935, but he never came close to showing that kind of form for the Red Sox.

Foxx was the game's most powerful right-handed slugger. He had already led the league in home runs three times, including a high of 58 in 1932, as well as taking the Triple Crown in 1933. The twenty-eight-year-old Jimmie was a good-natured, ever-smiling man, which was just as well, considering the brute strength he possessed. He was known as "the right-handed Babe Ruth," and people weren't kidding when they said it.

There were, and are, countless stories about Jimmie's power. "He could hit a ball as far as anybody," said Ted Lyons. "I don't know which stories in particular you've heard about his long-distance hitting, but I'd say you wouldn't go far wrong if you believed them all." Teammate Billy Werber vividly remembered one Foxx clout in Cleveland. "It went beyond the left field bleachers, which was four hundred seventeen feet. The bleachers ran up to a big Lux soap sign and beyond the sign was a very tall white oak tree. Foxx hit the ball through the top of that tree. We all jumped up in the dugout the moment he hit it to see where it was going. Dusty Cooke stood on the top step of the dugout gazing out toward left field for a few moments, then turned to me and said, 'It's a damned lie.' That ball must have gone close to six hundred feet."

Jimmie kept right on ripping when he joined Boston. In 1936 he batted .338, hit 41 home runs, and drove in 143 runs (and led in none of those departments; the American League was a very fast track in those years).

In January 1936 Yawkey peeled yet another top-line player from the Athletics roster when for a few players and "cash considerations" he picked up center fielder Roger (Doc) Cramer, a fine outfielder and at home plate the very model of consistency. Between 1932 and 1940 he never batted under .292 or over .336. The Sox also acquired infielder Eric McNair, who had the engaging nickname "Boob." A feisty little Mississippian, Boob liked to crowd the plate. There was a young pitcher in the league at that time named Robert Feller, all of seventeen years old and already in possession of the most fearsome fastball many living mortals had ever seen. Bob was not only quick, he was wild. One day McNair, leading off a game against Feller, was warned not to crowd the dish against the young man. "I don't give ground to no man," McNair replied. After strike 3 was announced by the umpire, McNair returned to the bench. His face was white. "Boys," he drawled, "from now on I'm giving young Mr. Feller all the room he wants. I don't mind getting bruised a bit. I don't even mind getting killed outright. But I'm damned if I'm going to be maimed for the rest of my life."

Wes Ferrell's eruptions were beginning to out-Grove Grove. One day Wes stalked off the mound in the middle of the game, upset at what he considered shabby support from his infield. Cronin announced a $1,000 fine and suspension. Wes refused to pay and just for good luck threatened to punch Joe in the jaw. No shots were fired, but in May 1937 Wes and his brother Rick, an excellent catcher and hitter (Rick was quiet and unoffending, the antithesis of his brother), were dealt to Washington for outfielder Ben Chapman and pitcher Bobo Newsom.

The Red Sox seemed intent upon collecting the league's singular characters. Bobo, traded more than fifteen times in his long career, was an irreverent sort. He earned his nickname by calling everyone "Bobo," including the game's nearest approximation to sainthood, Connie Mack. Bobo's days were numbered with the Red Sox, from day one. Whenever Cronin came over from shortstop to the mound to impart some managerial wisdom on the art of pitching, Newsom would stare disdainfully at him and ask, "Who's telling old Bobo how to pitch?" So after a half-season Newsom packed his bags and moved on to St. Louis, where he won 20 games.

Chapman, a talented ballplayer, was also quite a package. As a youngster with the Yankees he advised the aging Babe Ruth to retire before he got hurt, as this was no game "for an old man." Ben was hot-tempered and quick-fisted. He was also independent. One day he ignored a bunt sign, swung away, and rammed into a double play. His explanation to an in-

censed Cronin: "I don't bunt." So, despite a .340 batting average in 1938, Chapman was traded to Cleveland.

One by one the wave-makers left. Only Grove remained. Lefty was special. His outbursts, his intensity, his flinty personality, somehow they all exuded class. And he kept winning, long after his famed fastball had gone into the sunset. Year after year, working the mound with the smoothest mechanics in the league, Grove kept edging toward 300 victories. He won earned run average titles in 1935, 1936, 1938, and 1939, adding those four to the five he had taken with Philadelphia, giving him nine ERA crowns, far and away the best in the books, and one of the most impressive of all pitching records.

In 1938 the Red Sox had their best finish since 1918—second place, 9½ games behind a Yankee team they outhit by 25 points. Foxx bashed 50 homers, drove in 175 runs, batted .349. Jimmie was outhomered by Detroit's Hank Greenberg, who poled 58, but Foxx led in RBIs and batting, becoming only the second Red Sox player to win a batting title—Dale Alexander being the first in 1932. Cronin batted .325, third baseman Pinky Higgins .303, Chapman .340, Cramer .301, outfielder Joe Vosmik .324. The team, which batted .299 collectively, was undone by its pitching, again the familiar story. Right-hander Jim Bagby, son of a one-time 30-game winner with the Indians, was the ace with a 15–11 record. Righty Jack Wilson was 15–15; the thirty-eight-year-old Grove was 14–4.

Help was on the way, but not for the pitching staff. The pitchers seemed to go elsewhere—mostly to the Yankees in those days. The hitters came to Boston, and in 1939 the greatest of them all was about to sink his spikes into Fenway Park and unleash the purest, most flawless, most charismatic left-handed swing since the heyday of Babe Ruth.

Robert Moses (Lefty) Grove: a blazing fastball, with temper to match.

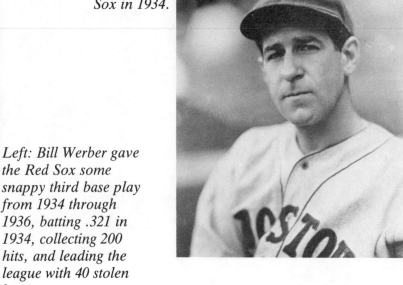

Right: Bucky Harris, manager of the Red Sox in 1934.

Left: Bill Werber gave the Red Sox some snappy third base play from 1934 through 1936, batting .321 in 1934, collecting 200 hits, and leading the league with 40 stolen bases.

Left to right, *Eddie Collins, Judge Landis, Tom Yawkey, Joe Cronin. They were in New York for the Yankees-Giants World Series in 1936.*

The Ferrell brothers, Wes (left) and Rick.

Below: Moe Berg, utility catcher for Boston from 1935 to 1939. One of the most erudite men ever to play big league ball, Moe spoke eight or nine languages, and it was said, could not hit the curve in any of them.

Left: A fine second baseman for Connie Mack for ten years, Max Bishop was about through when he got to Boston in 1934. He played for just two years.

Right: Outfielder Julius (Moose) Solters broke in with a .299 average with Boston in 1934, but a year later he was traded to the Browns.

It's spring training 1937 and Cronin is showing the boys how it's done.

Below: Eddie Morgan was a heavy-gunning first baseman with Cleveland. The Red Sox got him in 1934, Eddie batted .267 and was gone.

Right: Roger (Doc) Cramer. A sweetheart of a ballplayer, Doc played for the Sox for five years, batting .292, .305, .301, .311, .303— numbers typical of his twenty-year career.

Heinie Manush. This fine veteran outfielder played for the Red Sox in 1936, batting .291.

Southpaw Fritz Ostermuller. Fritz labored in the Fenway vineyards from 1934 through 1940. His best year was 1938, when he was 13–5.

Wes Ferrell. He won 25 in 1935, 20 a year later.

71

Jimmie Foxx crossing home plate after tagging a
long one, and one of his fans is so impressed
he's come out on the field to offer Jimmie a nip.
That's Joe Cronin looking the other way.

Jimmie Foxx

Ben Chapman, temperamental and talented. He batted .340 for the Red Sox in 1938, his only full year in Fenway, but was traded the next year.

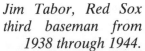

Jim Tabor, Red Sox third baseman from 1938 through 1944.

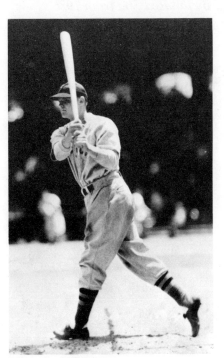

The Red Sox got out-fielder Joe Vosmik from the Browns in 1938. Joe batted .324 and led the league with 201 hits that year. He slumped off in 1939 and was sold to Brooklyn.

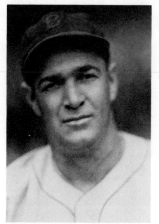

Right-hander Jim Bagby, Jr. He pitched for the Red Sox from 1938 through 1940 and again in 1946. He won 15 in 1938.

Bobo Newsom. He traveled from team to team like the wind. His brief stay in Boston in 1937 was productive—13–10.

Johnny Marcum pitched for Boston from 1936 through 1938. Thirteen wins in 1937 was his top mark.

Eric (Boob) McNair. This tough little infielder was employed by the Red Sox from 1936 through 1938. He hit .292 in 1937.

Above: Left-hander George (Rube) Walberg. He pitched for the Red Sox for four years (1934–37) after being acquired from the A's, mostly as a relief pitcher.

Jack Wilson was one of Boston's better pitchers in the late 1930s. He won 16 in 1937, 15 a year later. He was with the Sox from 1935 through 1941.

Jimmie Foxx, loosening up at the Red Sox spring training camp at Sarasota, Florida, March 1940.

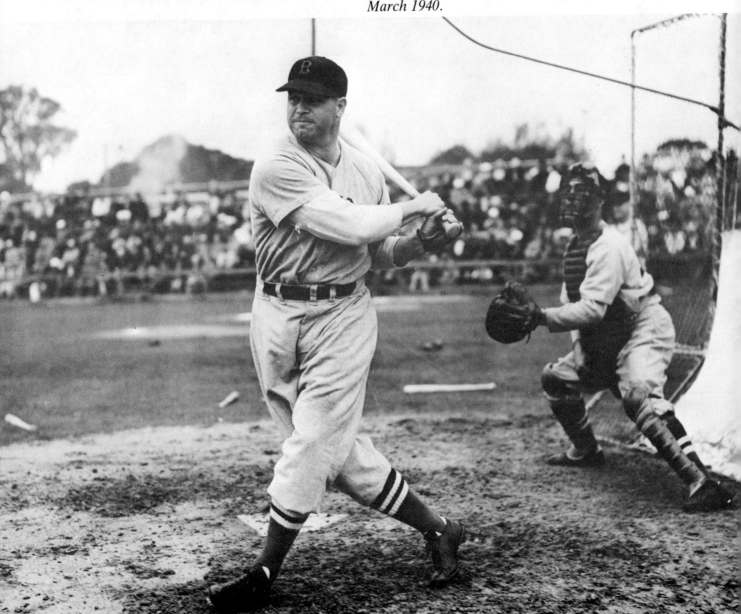

Right-hander Eldon Auker pitched just one year for the Red Sox, 1939, when he was 9–10. The former Detroit star was then traded to the Browns.

It's the skipper himself caught up in what sandlotters used to call "a pickle." Ganging up on Cronin are catcher Bill Dickey and third baseman Red Rolfe of the Yankees.

Johnny Peacock caught for the Red Sox from 1937 to 1944. He batted .303 in 1938.

Right-hander Joe Heving, who did some excellent relief pitching for the Red Sox from 1938 to 1940, logging records of 8–1, 11–3, 12–7. He was the younger brother of catcher John Heving.

First baseman-outfielder Lou Finney was obtained from the A's in 1939 and played for Boston until 1945. Lou batted .310 in 1939, .320 a year later.

5 · A LEGEND NAMED WILLIAMS

BACK IN THE LATE 1920s Joe McCarthy, then managing the Chicago Cubs, was asked by a young newspaperman to put together a composite of the perfect ball player. Joe listened patiently as the writer asked which players would represent which component of hitting, fielding, running, throwing, clutch play, and competitive zeal. Finally McCarthy said, "Why don't you just say Frank Frisch and be done with it?"

And so shall we put together the components of the perfect hitter? They would include power, judgment, timing, eyesight, coordination, patience, self-discipline, and the burning desire to excel. *Why don't you just say Ted Williams and be done with it?* All right. And now take all of the crucial ingredients, pack them into Williams, and then add a picture-perfect swing, the good looks of a Malibu Beach rascal, a magnetic personality, and a good dose of grainy temperament to keep him from ever being dull, and you have "The Thumper," "The Splendid Splinter," a man who grew up to fulfill his boyhood ambition "to be the greatest hitter that ever lived."

Was he indeed the greatest hitter? How do you determine the indeterminable? Once you begin trying, the heights become dramatic, the air rarefied. The candidates thin out to a mere handful. There is Ruth (there is always Ruth), and there is, by unanimous testimony of his contemporaries, Shoeless Joe Jackson, and there is Rogers Hornsby, he of the imperial batting averages. And there is Ted Williams. Drop the four into a barrel, reach in and lift one out and chances are you will have the greatest hitter that ever lived. In other words, the differences are so slight as to be meaningless. But Ruth, Jackson, and Hornsby were at

one time contemporaneous. Jackson left the game in 1920, while Ruth and Hornsby had their heyday years in the 1920s. Since that time, when it comes to hitting, no name has been mentioned in the same breath as Williams's—not Foxx's nor Gehrig's nor DiMaggio's nor Musial's nor Aaron's nor Carew's. Put bluntly, Williams has been acclaimed unchallengeably the greatest hitter for more than half a century. It may be argued until the moon turns to cream cheese, but it is quite likely that no one, not Ruth nor anyone else, was Williams's equal at home plate when it came to the pure, unvarnished art of mashing a baseball. And for twenty-two years, from 1939 through 1960, he belonged exclusively to the Boston Red Sox.

It began in 1936, in San Diego. Red Sox general manager Eddie Collins was on a scouting trip to have a look at San Diego second baseman Bobby Doerr, on whom the Sox had taken an option. Collins liked what he saw of Doerr, and he also saw someone else. Watching the big, lanky, left-handed-swinging kid in the batting cage made the old second baseman's eyes pop. Eddie went to Bill Lane, owner of the club, and said the Red Sox would pick up the option on Doerr. Then he asked about the other boy. So obscure was the youngster—he had hardly played any games yet—that Lane at first did not know whom Collins was referring to. When Eddie explained, Lane said, "Oh, Williams. Hell, he's just out of high school. Just seventeen years old. Give him a few years."

Collins, however, refused to be deterred. He got Lane to give him an option on Williams's contract. In 1937, his first full year in pro ball, Ted batted .291 and hit 23 home runs. Not particularly overwhelming statistics; but the thing about the youngster was, every time you saw him he seemed to be getting better. Overanxious at first, he began becoming more and more selective at the plate, slowly but keenly honing that judgment of a pitched ball that ultimately became so fine that in his later years umpires were known to call a close pitch a ball simply because Williams had not offered at it.

He went to spring training with the Red Sox in 1938, the most cockily self-confident rookie anyone had seen in a long time. Doerr, now established as the club's second baseman, tried to take his former teammate down a peg by saying, "Wait till you see Foxx hit." And young Theodore reportedly said, "Wait till Foxx sees *me* hit." Williams denies having said it, though adding, "But I suppose it wouldn't have been unlike me."

Boston had an all-.300-hitting outfield in Ben Chapman, Doc Cramer, and Joe Vosmik. With this outfield alignment already in place, the club decided to give Williams another year of seasoning at Minneapolis, hoping he would improve his fielding, an aspect of the game the bat-conscious youngster had been willfully ignoring.

The twenty-year-old Teddy gave Minneapolis fans a year to remember. He batted .366, hit 43 home runs, drove in 142 runs. Next stop: Boston.

"Ted was a great boy," Doc Cramer recalled. "I liked him. That first spring he was with the team, we were coming up from the South, heading for Boston. We stopped off in Atlanta to play a game with the Atlanta Crackers. Ted was playing right field. Somebody hit the ball out to him, and it went between his legs, all the way to the wall. He chased it down, mad as the dickens at himself for missing it, and when he got to it, he picked it up and just threw that ball over the right field fence—right through Sears, Roebuck's plate glass window, we learned later on.

"I was there alongside him when he threw it. I had to hold my hand over my mouth to keep from laughing. Then I looked around and sure enough, he was coming—Cronin. Walking out from shortstop, ver-r-ry slow.

"So I said, 'Ted, here comes Cronin. Now keep your mouth shut. Don't say anything. *Yes* him. That's all there is to it.'

"Cronin didn't say much. Wasn't much he could say. He just took Ted right out of there and sat him on the bench. It didn't bother Ted too much, except he wanted to stay in and hit. That boy loved to hit. With good reason.

"Cronin said to me a few days later, 'I want you to take Ted out and teach him to field.' I said all right. So I had him out there with somebody hitting them to him. He'd miss one, catch one, then miss a couple more. Finally he said, 'Ah, Doc, the hell with this. They don't pay off on me catching these balls. They're gonna pay me to hit. That's what they're gonna do.'

"And I said, 'Well, I can see that, Ted. They're gonna pay you to hit.' There was no trouble seeing that. He had that swing."

Yankee outfielder Tommy Henrich remembered the first time the Yankees saw Williams in 1939. "We had a clubhouse meeting before our first series with the Red Sox. We talked about Cronin, Foxx, going down their lineup. We get around to Williams. What do we know about Williams? Spud Chandler wants to know. He's pitching. Well, the consensus was pitch him high and tight, low and away. The old words of wisdom. So we went out and played. And Ted had a pretty good day. The next day we're talking again. What did we learn about Williams? Chandler speaks up.

"'Well, I'll tell you what I found out,' he says. 'High and tight is ball one, and low and away is ball two.'

"Then Bill Dickey, in his own quiet way, said, 'Boys, he's just a damned good hitter.'

"And that sizes up Ted Williams. That's what we found out, after one look. And it stuck."

He batted .327 in his rookie year, hit 31 home runs, and led the league with 145 runs batted in. He teamed with Jimmie Foxx (.360 batting average, 35 homers) to give the Red Sox the most potent one-two punch in the league. In addition, Doerr batted .318, Cronin .308, Cramer .311. Overall, the club batted .291, highest in the league, but still finished 17 games behind the Yankees. Again, it was lack of pitching, with the thirty-nine-year-old Grove leading the staff with a 15–4 record. No one else won more than 11.

In 1940 the Sox broke their own attendance record by selling 716,000 tickets, but the best the fans could get for their money was a fourth-place finish despite the highest team batting average in the league, .286. It was the third straight time Boston had topped the league in batting and still had no cigar to show for it.

It was a no-nonsense attack, too, with five men clouting 20 or more homers—Foxx (36), Cronin (24), Williams (23), Doerr (22), Jim Tabor (21). With the exception of Tabor, they all drove in over 100 runs. Williams showed he was for real with a .344 average, which twenty years later would turn out to be precisely his lifetime average.

As if they didn't have enough punch in the lineup, the Red Sox in 1940 added another .300 bat. It belonged to a studious-looking twenty-three-year-old center fielder with almost flawless defensive skills and a familiar name: DiMaggio, first name Dominic.

Dominic was the youngest of the ballplaying DiMaggios, and the smallest. Because of his size and comparative lack of power—the rap against him was "he only hits singles"—most big league clubs ignored him despite some solid .300 seasons in the Pacific Coast League. But he was simply too good a ballplayer to be ignored for long, and as a matter of fact the Red Sox reportedly shelled out something like $75,000 to get him.

It wasn't much different in 1941, except this time it was more interesting. The club led in batting for a fourth straight time with a .283 mark. It was good enough to elevate them to second place, but that was almost the same as heading up the second division, since they finished 17 games behind a Yankee club that batted 14 points lower and scored fewer runs than the Red Sox but that had pitching to burn— their sixth starter, Ernie Bonham, had a lower ERA than anybody on the Red Sox staff. There was, finally, one notable addition to the Boston pitching corps, Cecil (Tex) Hughson. A tall, handsome Texan with a live fastball, the young right-hander broke in with a 5–3 record.

The difference for the Red Sox and their fans in 1941 lay in several individual perfor-

mances. The first occurred in the All-Star game at Detroit on July 8. With the National League seemingly on its way to a victory, Williams came to bat in the last of the ninth with two on and two out. Claude Passeau of the Chicago Cubs was on the mound. The Cub righty, who had fanned Williams an inning before, came in with a belt-high fastball and Teddy swung. "An all-out home run swing," he remembered. "Probably with my eyes shut." It was a shot that carried far up into the right field stands and became the most dramatic home run in All-Star game history, sending a long, warm electric current of pride through all of New England.

Two weeks later, on July 25, there was another memorable event. This time it took place in Fenway Park. It did not have the exultant suddenness of Williams's home run; this had the mellowed sweetness of inevitability. This story had, in fact, its beginning sixteen years before, when Robert Moses Grove was a twenty-five-year-old rookie with the Athletics. It was now sixteen years and 299 victories later and the silver-haired forty-one-year-old left-hander was about to incise his name alongside those of Walter Johnson, Christy Mathewson, Grover Cleveland Alexander, and Eddie Plank—up to that point the only pitchers to win 300 or more games in the twentieth century.

Laboring through a sweltering 90-degree day, Grove won his 300th and final game (he retired at season's end with a 7–7 record and 300–141 lifetime) by a 10–6 score.

There was one more moment of historic proportions for Red Sox fans in 1941, and it came on the final day of the season, though it had been building all summer long, day by day, hit by hit. Again it was Williams, again with that flair for the dramatic that is part of the chemistry and the distinction and the isolation of greatness.

Overshadowed that summer by Joe DiMaggio's 56-game hitting streak, Williams had been pounding away at a .400 pace. The last .400 hitter had been Bill Terry of the New York Giants in 1930; the last .400 hitter in the American League had been Detroit's Harry Heilmann in 1923, at that time the fourth .400 average in four years. Williams came down to the final day batting .400 on the nose, with a doubleheader scheduled against the A's in Philadelphia.

Cronin offered to sit Williams down, saying no one would blame Ted for it. But Williams, alive with the bravado and self-confidence of a supremely gifted twenty-three-year-old, and, like any great athlete, stimulated by the blood lust of a challenge, insisted he would play. As Williams approached the plate for the first time, umpire Bill McGowan said to him, "To hit .400 a batter has got to be loose. He has got to be loose."

If Williams had been any looser he would have fallen apart. He played both games, connected for six hits in eight at bats, and pushed his final average up to .406, where it remains the highest figure in more than six decades, an Everest of digits that no one has since been able to scale.

In 1942 the Sox led in batting for the fifth straight time and again finished second, this time 9 games behind the Yankees. Williams won his second straight batting title with a .356 mark, enjoying the luxury of a 50-point drop and still coming out on top. He also led with 36 home runs and 137 runs batted in, thus winning the first of his two Triple Crowns.

The club added rookie shortstop Johnny Pesky to the lineup in 1942, Cronin relegating himself to part-time status. Pesky, aptly named, was a singles hitter with a .300 eye. Johnny led in hits with 205 and batted .331, second in the league to Williams.

There was a further changing of the guard in 1942. On June 1 first baseman Jimmie Foxx, who had performed nobly for the Red Sox since 1936, was waived to the Chicago Cubs. Jimmie's departure began a revolving door policy at first base for Boston that would plague them for decades.

The 1942 season finally saw some quality pitching arrive on the Fenway mound. Tex Hughson blossomed into an ace, winning 22 and losing 6, leading the league in wins and strikeouts. Broadway Charlie Wagner, a personable right-hander with a fashion-plate wardrobe, was 14–11 and Joe Dobson, a burly righty, was 11–9. After that, however, the staff thinned out perceptibly.

A year later the full impact of the war struck

baseball. Like all other clubs, the Red Sox saw their roster depleted by departures to military service. Williams, Pesky, and Dom DiMaggio were gone by the time the 1943 season opened. Hughson and Doerr left late in the 1944 season, Hughson with a 17–5 record, Doerr with a .325 batting average that Cleveland's Lou Boudreau beat out by 2 points for the batting championship.

Fielding a patchwork lineup typical of the war years, Cronin's men finished seventh in 1943, fourth in 1944, and seventh again in 1945. The only bright spot for Boston during those dreary years was the performance in 1945 of Dave Ferriss, a twenty-three-year-old right-hander. Known as "Boo," Ferriss had been discharged from the Army because of an asthmatic condition. Originally ticketed for the top farm club at Louisville in the American Association, Dave made the big club and broke in with two shutout victories. Immensely popular with Fenway fans because of a shy, likable personality, Ferriss logged a 21–10 record working for a seventh-place club. Not since Wes Ferrell had done it with Cleveland in 1929 had an American League rookie won 20 games. It made Red Sox fans, those incurable believers, want to look ahead to 1946.

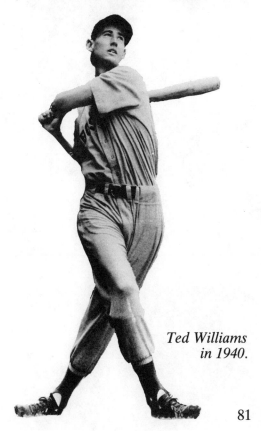

Ted Williams in 1940.

81

A smiling Ted Williams crosses the plate after his dramatic ninth-inning home run in the 1941 All-Star game. Extending his hand to Ted is Joe DiMaggio. Joe Gordon is in the background. No. 30 is Detroit coach Mervin Shea.

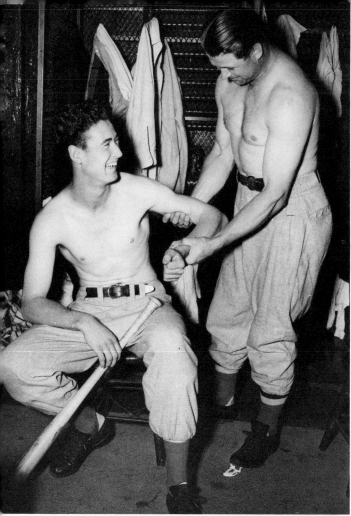

Red Sox rookie center fielder Dom DiMaggio in 1940. He played until 1953, retiring with a .298 lifetime average. His top average was .328 in 1950, the year his 15 stolen bases were good enough to lead the league.

Jimmie Foxx squeezing, trying to find out how the slender Williams is able to generate such power.

Ervin (Pete) Fox, one of the league's steadier hitting outfielders with Detroit in the 1930s, was acquired by Boston in 1941. Pete batted .302 in 1941 and .315 in 1944.

Sandlot star Bobby Doerr, just before he signed with Hollywood of the Pacific Coast League in 1934 at the age of sixteen.

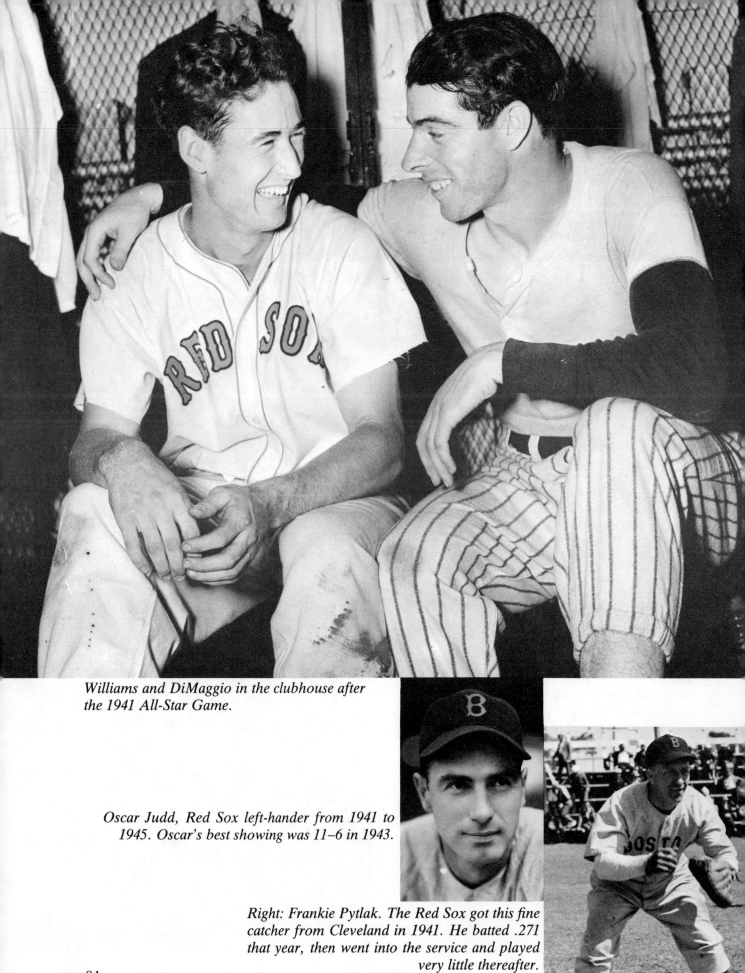

Williams and DiMaggio in the clubhouse after the 1941 All-Star Game.

Oscar Judd, Red Sox left-hander from 1941 to 1945. Oscar's best showing was 11–6 in 1943.

Right: Frankie Pytlak. The Red Sox got this fine catcher from Cleveland in 1941. He batted .271 that year, then went into the service and played very little thereafter.

84

Below: Bobby Doerr, Boston's all-time second baseman. He played from 1937 through 1951, leaving with a lifetime mark of .288, with a high of .325 in 1944.

Johnny Pesky, real name Paveskovich. He played seven full years for Boston and batted over .300 in six of them. He led the league in hits his first three years, 1942, 1946, 1947. He managed the club in 1963 and 1964.

Dick Newsome, a thirty-year-old rookie right-hander who surprised everyone by winning 19 and losing 10 in 1941. He dropped to 8 wins in each of the next two seasons, then was released.

The face of a 300-game winner. Lefty Grove in 1941.

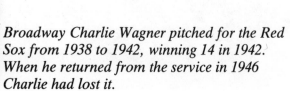

Broadway Charlie Wagner pitched for the Red Sox from 1938 to 1942, winning 14 in 1942. When he returned from the service in 1946 Charlie had lost it.

Tex Hughson in 1941. He was 22–6 in 1942, 18–5 in 1944, 20–11 in 1946. Finished by a sore arm in 1949, he left behind a 96–54 lifetime record.

Williams and Doerr

Ted Williams completing a familiar journey in April 1942 after busting one against the A's. Giving him the glad hand is Jimmie Foxx, while Johnny Pesky awaits.

Williams in training as a Marine pilot in the winter of 1942.

Another member of Boston's wartime outfield, Johnny Lazor batted .310 in 1945.

George (Catfish) Metkovich. He played the outfield and first base for the Red Sox from 1943 through 1946.

Veteran slugger Bob Johnson wound up his career with the Red Sox in 1944–45. He batted .324 in 1944, .280 the next year. He had been one of the league's fine power hitters with the Athletics through the 1930s.

89

Dave Ferriss

Below: Leon Culberson, Red Sox outfielder from 1943 through 1947. He batted .313 as a part-timer in 1946.

Above: Tom McBride, Red Sox outfielder from 1943 to 1947. Tom batted .305 in 1945 and .301 in 1946.

6 · A PENNANT, FINALLY

WHEN THE GUNS FINALLY STOPPED FIRING and the war ended, the big leaguers returned. Williams, Doerr, Pesky, Dom DiMaggio, Hughson, Dobson, and the rest returned to Fenway, still young, willing, and able. After second-place finishes in 1941 and 1942, Red Sox fans were thirsting for their first pennant since 1918, and Tom Yawkey, patient but frustrated since 1933, said it was about time. The pressure was on Cronin; going into his twelfth season as skipper, it was do-or-die for the now overweight former great who had played his last game in 1945.

For once there was an array of strong arms on the mound. Hughson, Ferriss, Dobson, and southpaw Mickey Harris gave the Sox a solid front line of starters. There was some bullpen talent too, in lefty Earl Johnson and National League pickup Bob Klinger.

The gap at first base had been plugged solidly, if temporarily, by the acquisition of veteran slugger Rudy York from Detroit in a swap for shortstop Eddie Lake, made expendable by the return of Pesky. There were problems at third base and in right field. Neither was ever satisfactorily solved, with six men performing at third during the year and another variety rotating through right field.

But the lack of total balance made little difference, for this turned out to be an unstoppable Red Sox team. They broke out of the starting gate with a vengeance. From late April into the second week of May, they put together the longest winning streak in club history, 15 games. Winning 21 of their firsst 25, they were on their way.

Williams swung the bat as if he hadn't missed a day, hitting .342 and belting 38 home runs. Pesky, also back from a three-year hiatus, again led the league in hits and batted .335. York and Doerr each drove in over 100 runs.

Dave Ferriss proved he was no wartime wonder by posting a 25–6 record. Hughson was 20–11, Harris 17–9, Dobson 13–7. It was the best Red Sox pitching staff in nearly thirty years.

Once again Williams dominated the All-Star game, fittingly enough played in Fenway that year. This time there were no last-minute dramatics, just an exhibition of power hitting, topped off by one of the game's more memorable serio-comic moments.

Pittsburgh's Rip Sewell was on the mound for the National League when Williams came to bat in the last of the eighth inning. Ted had already singled twice and homered, leading the American League to an 8–0 advantage. Sewell was known for his "blooper" pitch, a big, slow, nothing ball that he occasionally lobbed up to the plate from out of an arc of around 25 feet. Rip had uncanny control of this parachute pitch. Years later he reminisced about the day the blooper ball was sent on its furthest ride.

"Before the game, Ted said to me, 'Hey, Rip, you wouldn't throw that damned crazy pitch in a game like this, would you?'

"'Sure,' I said. 'I'm gonna throw it to you.'

"'Man, he said, 'don't throw that ball in a game like this.'

"'I'm gonna throw it to you, Ted,' I said. 'So look out.'

"Well, if you remember that game, they had us beat eight to nothing going into the last of the eighth. It was a lousy game, and the fans were bored. I was pitching that inning, and Ted came to bat. You know how Ted used to be up there at the plate, all business. I smiled

91

at him. He must've recalled our conversation because he shook his head from side to side in quick little movements, telling me not to throw it. I nodded to him: You're gonna get it, buddy. He shook his head again. And I nodded to him again. He was gonna get it. So I wound up like I was going to throw a fastball, and here comes the blooper. He swung from Port Arthur and just fouled it on the tip of his bat.

"He stepped back in, staring out at me, and I nodded to him again: You're gonna get another one. I threw him another one, but it was outside and he let it go. Now he was looking for it. Well, I threw him a fastball and he didn't like that. Surprised him. Now I had him one ball, two strikes. I wound up and threw him another blooper. It was a good one. Dropping right down the chute for a strike. He took a couple of steps up on it—which was the right way to attack that pitch, incidentally—and he hit it right out of there. And I mean he *hit* it.

"Well, the fans stood up, and they went crazy. I got a standing ovation when I walked off the mound after that inning. We'd turned a dead turkey of a ball game into a real crowd pleaser.

"And he was the only man ever to hit a home run off the blooper, Ted Williams in the '46 All-Star game."

A few weeks later Williams again was the center of an unorthodox move on a baseball diamond. After the first game of a double-header against the Indians, during which he hammered 3 home runs and drove in 8 runs in an 11–10 Boston victory, Ted found himself faced with a radically new defensive alignment in the second game. Frustrated by Williams' barrage, Cleveland manager Lou Boudreau had devised what became known as the "Boudreau shift."

When Ted came to bat in the second game he found the Cleveland fielders packing the right side of the diamond. The right fielder and first baseman positioned themselves close to the foul line. The second baseman moved closer to first and back on the outfield grass. The shortstop (Boudreau) took up the second baseman's normal position. The third baseman placed himself directly behind second base.

The center fielder stood in right-center. The left fielder remained the only man on the left side of the diamond, in short left-center. The alignment gave the pull-hitting Williams the entire left side of the field to shoot at, if he so desired.

Boudreau was counting on Williams' pride and stubbornness. And he was right. Even as the shift, with various modifications, caught on around the league, he continued to swing directly into it. How many hits it cost him will never be known. Still, he took four more batting titles, lost another by a fraction of a point, and ended with a .344 lifetime average. Take away the shift, which no batter before him had ever faced, add the five prime years he lost to military service, and the scintillating lifetime statistics he put in the book are even more impressive.

It looked like a pennant-clinching by Labor Day, but then the club fell into a slump. Finally, on September 13, the inevitable took place. Hughson hurled a 1–0 nifty to nail it down. Ironically, the one run came on an inside-the-park homer by Williams—the only one of his career—when Ted decided to clip a pitch into the yawning left field gap opened up by the shift.

In the National League, the St. Louis Cardinals had taken their fourth pennant in five years. Not noted for power, they were a club whose strength lay in pitching, speed, defense, and timely hitting. The squad included the National League's best hitter, Stan Musial, Enos Slaughter, Terry Moore, Marty Marion, Red Schoendienst, and an array of other greyhounds, all graduates of the Cardinal farm system.

The Series was billed as a match-up between Williams and Musial. As so often hppens in a World Series, however, the accolades went to someone of lesser stature. Williams connected for just 5 singles and batted .200, while Stan the Man batted .222, although numbering 4 doubles and a triple among his 6 hits.

The star of the Series turned out to be a crafty, thin-faced St. Louis southpaw named Harry (The Cat) Breechen. After Boston took the opener in ten innings in St. Louis 3–2 on York's homer, Breechen came back in Game

Two with a 4-hit shutout victory, 3–0. Ferriss blanked the Cardinals 4–0 in Game Three, but the next day the Cardinals opened up on the Red Sox pitching with a 12–3 win. Boston went up three games to two the next day behind Dobson, 6–3.

The two clubs then entrained for St. Louis, the Red Sox with the taste of a world championship in their mouths. But the hero of Game Two, Harry Breechen, made it a seven-game Series by stopping the Sox once more, 4–1. The stage was set for the finale, and for the most thrilling basepath dash in Series history.

It was Ferriss against Cardinal righty Murray

Dickson. The Cards broke a 1–1 tie with 2 in the bottom of the fifth. The Red Sox tied it in the top of the eighth. Pinch-hitters Rip Russell and George Metkovich opened with a single and double respectively. At this point Cardinal manager Eddie Dyer lifted Dickson and, to everyone's surprise, brought in Breechen, who had pitched a complete game victory the day before. Harry was not a robust fellow, but also he was not a power pitcher, relying mainly on control and a devilish screwball.

Breechen retired Wally Moses and Johnny Pesky without allowing a runner to advance. But then Dom DiMaggio ripped a double to right, scoring both runners and tying the game.

Ted Williams, back from the wars.

In running out his hit, however, Dom pulled a muscle and had to be replaced by a pinch-runner, Leon Culberson. The injury was soon to become crucially significant.

Cronin brought Bob Klinger in to pitch the last of the eighth. Enos Slaughter touched Klinger for a single, but the ex-National League righty retired the next two men. The batter was Harry (The Hat) Walker, a left-handed spray hitter. With Slaughter breaking, Walker lined a hit to left-center. Culberson, playing in place of the sure-handed DiMaggio in center, did not play the ball cleanly. Meanwhile, Slaughter, an aggressive player whose nonstop hustle was legendary, was rip-roaring around the bases as over 36,000 Cardinal fans came to their feet exhorting him on. Third base coach Mike Gonzalez threw up the "stop" sign, but Enos ignored it. He had made up his mind he was going all the way.

When Culberson's relay reached Pesky, Bobby Doerr shouted to him to go home with it. But the volume of noise was too great. Pesky hesitated for just a split second—just long enough to allow himself to be fitted with goat's horns—and then to his great surprise saw the Slaughter Express barreling for home. Whether the hesitation was that crucial is debatable, but in any event Johnny's throw to the plate was too late.

The Red Sox threatened in the ninth but Breechen refused to give in, shutting them down and gaining his third win of the Series. The first Red Sox World Series in twenty-eight years was over. If someone had told Sox fans then that that would be it for another twenty-one years, there would have been hoots of derision and disbelief.

What happened in 1947 was that the finest Red Sox pitching staff since the World War I era came up with bad arms. Ferris and Hughson were slowed to 12–11 records each, while Mickey Harris dropped to 5–4. For all intents and purposes, each ceased being a factor on the Fenway mound. Only Dobson, with an 18–8 record, was effective.

The club dropped to third place and Boston fans had to settle for glorying in Ted Williams' bat all summer. The Kid took his second Triple Crown with a .343 batting average, 32 home

runs, and 114 runs batted in. As an indication of the awe in which he was held by pitchers, he also accumulated a mammoth 162 bases on balls, second in history to Ruth's 170 in 1923. And it was on June 13 of that year that night ball came to Fenway.

The year also marked the end of the Cronin era. After thirteen years as field boss, by far the longest managerial tenure in club history, the old shortstop stepped aside. Cronin moved up to become general manager, replacing Eddie Collins, who was retiring because of poor health.

Replacing Cronin was another Irishman named Joe—Joe McCarthy, long-time skipper of Boston's archrival and nemesis, the New York Yankees. Joe had quit the Yankees in early 1946 after the most successful managerial regime in history because of a combination of ill health and a dislike for team co-owner Larry MacPhail. After two seasons of fidgeting on the sidelines, McCarthy was back.

One of the first questions that occurred to Boston writers and fans after the hiring of McCarthy was, would the disciplinarian skipper be able to get along with his star slugger Williams? What some people may have overlooked was that Joe over a long career was no novice to superstar quality and temperament, having managed Rogers Hornsby, Babe Ruth, Lou Gehrig, and Joe DiMaggio. When the question was put to him, McCarthy gave a classic response: "Any manager who can't get along with a .400 hitter ought to have his head examined." And as a matter of fact, the two got along without the least hint of discord. Williams later remarked, "Joe McCarthy was something special. I loved Joe McCarthy." And on Joe's part: "Williams was no problem. He played. He hustled. Followed orders. He followed orders perfectly. Of course I only gave him one order—hit. No insubordination there. He hit."

In November 1947 the Red Sox swung a couple of massive "pennant insurance" trades with the St. Louis Browns, a perennially depressed area in the league. The Browns, who lost ball games and money in equal measure, occasionally came up with a good ballplayer. In 1947 they had a few; in 1948 they had fewer, thanks to Tom Yawkey's always-willing checkbook.

For cash estimated to be around $375,000 and a battalion of players that included infielders Eddie Pellagrini, Sam Dente, and Bill Sommers; outfielder Pete Layden; catchers Roy Partee and Don Palmer; pitchers Jim Wilson, Clem Dreisewerd, Al Widmar, and Joe Ostrowski, the Red Sox received the pick of the Browns rosters. Eastward ho came slugging shortstop Vern Stephens, utility infielder Billy Hitchcock and right-handers Jack Kramer and Ellis Kinder.

Kramer and Kinder were expected to pick up the slack left by the sore arms of Hughson, Ferriss, and Harris. Stephens added another bicep to an already muscular lineup. His arrival caused McCarthy to switch Pesky to third, a move some observers thought might have been better had it been done the other way around.

In addition to Stephens, the club added another sharp bat that belonged to twenty-two-year-old rookie Billy Goodman. A line drive hitter with a .300 cut, Goodman ranks among the most outstanding utility men in baseball history. He played first, second, third, and the outfield with equal proficiency. In 1950, dividing his time between the infield and outfield, he won a batting crown with a .354 mark. He was a gem to have on anyone's ball club—versatile, talented, uncomplaining. He played in Boston from 1948 to 1956 and never batted under .293. In his rookie year, most of which he played at first base, Goodman batted .310. The year before, Billy had come up for a look-see, getting into a few games, mostly as a pinch-hitter. One day Cronin sent him in as a pinch-hitter with the admonition, "Make him throw you two strikes." The pitcher was Bob Feller. "I did better," Billy recalled. "I made him throw me three."

The '48 club had Goodman at first, Doerr at second, Stephens at short, Pesky at third; in the outfield Williams, DiMaggio, and veteran Stan Spence; behind the plate another veteran, George (Birdie) Tebbetts. Kramer gave the Red Sox one year of dividends for the bankroll they expended on him, going 18–5, while Dobson was 16–10, Kinder 10–7, reliever Earl Johnson 10–4, and a fine-looking young south-

paw named Mel Parnell was 15–8. Williams ripped away for one of his finest years, .369 (his fourth batting title), with 25 long ones and 127 runs batted in.

It all added up to something unprecedented in American League history—a first-place tie. At the end of 154 games the Sox and the Indians had identical 96–58 records, two games ahead of the third-place Yankees. League rules called for a one-game playoff.

Boston won the coin flip and the game was played in Fenway Park on October 4. The Indians started their rookie sensation, left-handed knuckleballer Gene Bearden. McCarthy, in perhaps the most controversial decision of his career, went with veteran right-hander Denny Galehouse. "I didn't have anybody else," Joe said. "My front-line starters were all used up. I could have started Parnell or Kinder or one of the others, but then I would have been second-guessed for starting a tired pitcher. No matter what you do," Joe said philosophically, "you get second-guessed."

It probably would have made no difference whom the Red Sox started, for that day they were up against a raging, unstoppable force named Lou Boudreau. The Cleveland shortstop-manager was always a sterling clutch performer, and this day his adrenalin count was at record levels. "Managing like mad," in Red Smith's memorable phrase, Boudreau hit 2 home runs and 2 singles to back up Bearden's steady pitching and led his club to an 8–3 pennant-winning victory.

If 1948 was tough medicine for Red Sox fans, then 1949 was worse, for they again lost the pennant in the season's final game, but this time it was to the despised Yankees.

It was Casey Stengel's first year of magic and manipulation in New York and the old wizard seemed to be doing it with mirrors. His injury-riddled Yankees were outhit in almost every offensive department by the Red Sox, but still came out on top.

Some of Stengel's magic was named Raschi, Reynolds, Lopat, Byrne, and Page, a marvelous array of pitchers. Some of it was named Berra, Henrich, Rizzuto, Bauer, and Woodling. And a large measure of it was named DiMaggio, Joseph.

Williams' only rival for The Game's Greatest Player accolade had missed the first 65 games of the season due to a heel injury when he joined his club in Fenway at the end of June for a three-game series. What he did in Boston in those three games ranks high in the DiMaggio legend, a notch under his 56-game hitting streak. With nothing more than a few batting practice sessions to warm his bat, Joe strode into Boston pitching with uncompromising savagery, hitting 4 home runs (3 of them game-winners) and driving in 9 runs.

The Yankee sweep seemed to have a demoralizing effect on the Sox. By July 4 Boston was 12½ games behind. But then McCarthy got them revved up and they went on a tear, smashing the league apart and winning 58 of their next 77. As they prepared for their two final games of the season they held a 1-game lead over the Yankees. Those two games were scheduled to be played at Yankee Stadium, traditionally a meat-grinder for pennant pretenders.

All year long the Sox had been led by two marvelous performers on the mound—Parnell with a 25–7 season and Kinder who finished at 23–6. The lineup bristled with base hits that summer. Williams had another titanic season, batting .343 and leading with 43 home runs and tying Stephens with 159 runs batted in, losing an unprecedented third Triple Crown by two-tenths of a point to Detroit's George Kell. Doerr batted .309, Dom DiMag .307, Goodman .298, Pesky .306, and early-season acquisition (from the Browns) Al Zarilla .281.

The Yankees won the Saturday game 5–4, thanks to a superb relief stint by Joe Page, who had been doing it all season long. So the stage was set for Sunday. Not since 1904, when Jack Chesbro had wild-pitched Boston to a pennant, had these two rivals cut it so fine.

The opposing pitchers were New York's big, gutty, right-hander, Vic Raschi, a 20-game winner, and Boston's Ellis Kinder, noted equally for his capacity to hold whisky and for his swooping curve balls.

The Yankees edged out to a 1–0 lead in the bottom of the first, and then Raschi and Kinder locked into a grim duel before over 70,000 witnesses, keeping this the 1–0 game

the drama almost demanded it be. In the top of the eighth, still trailing by a run, McCarthy was forced to hit for Kinder. Boston did not score. Parnell came in to pitch the last of the eighth. He yielded a home run to Tommy Henrich, a single to Berra, and was gone. Tex Hughson, at career's end now (literally; this was his final big league appearance), came in and loaded the bases. Jerry Coleman then delivered the key blow, a sinking, softly hit liner to right that Al Zarilla dove for and missed by inches. By the time the ball was retrieved, three more Yankee runs had scored, giving the New Yorkers a 5–0 lead.

Boston fought back for three runs in the top of the ninth, but fell short. A disconsolate Red Sox team headed back to Boston before scattering for the winter. They were met at South Station by thousands of representatives of that inextinguishable breed known as Red Sox fans, come to cheer and console and assure their heroes that next year would be *the* year.

But it wasn't. After winning 48 games between them, Parnell slipped to 18–10, Kinder to 14–12. Dobson won 15 and young lefty Chuck Stobbs 12. Another young southpaw, Mickey McDermott, a twenty-one-year-old with a big league fastball and lovably breezy personality, was 7–3.

The hitting was more awesome than ever, the Sox adding the steaming bat of a giant first baseman, Walt Dropo. The twenty-seven-year-old muscle man batted .322, hit 34 home runs, and tied Stephens for the RBI lead with 144. (Walt wasn't really that good though. McCarthy spotted some flaws in his swing and in due time so did the rest of the league. Dropo, who broke in looking like the new Jimmie Foxx, was traded to Detroit two years later.) Pesky batted .312, Zarilla .325, Dom DiMaggio .328, Tebbetts .310, Stephens .295, Doerr .294, and utility man Goodman .354 while playing all over the map, but still accumulating enough at bats to win the batting title.

Williams had another All-Star game experience of note, this time painfully unpleasant. Ted shattered his left elbow making a spectacular catch at Comiskey Park. He got into just 89 games, batted .317, hit 28 home runs, and drove in 97 of his buddies—better than a one-per-game average.

On June 7 and 8 the club unleashed the most frightening two-game attack in modern baseball history, burying the Browns by scores of 20–4 and 29–4, the latter total the most runs ever blasted across by a team in a single game.

Despite this explosive hitting, the Sox were barely at .500 after their first 62 games. At this point, a tired and weary Joe McCarthy resigned and retired from baseball. "I guess it begins to catch up to you," Joe said later. "I began to feel I wasn't a good manager anymore. So I quit."

The new manager was Steve O'Neill, a rotund former catcher who had skippered Cleveland and Detroit. Steve led the club to a third-place finish in 1950 and again in 1951, after which he was replaced by Lou Boudreau. When Boudreau took over he announced at his press conference that the club would make every effort to win another pennant, that there were no untouchables on the roster, not even Williams. That looked good in the papers the next day, but it was really a lot of canned heat—there was no way that Yawkey would ever let his .400 hitter leave Boston.

A year later, however, Williams did leave the club for two years, but it was under the call of a stronger authority—he was called up from the inactive Reserves by the Marines after the outbreak of the Korean War. At the age of thirty-three, Williams was having two more prime years gouged from his career.

Also leaving the club was Bobby Doerr, the club's all-time second baseman. Doerr retired after the 1951 season because of a bad back. Through a fourteen-year career he batted .288.

CHANGING OF THE GUARD

In 1952 the club underwent a major face-lifting, thanks to a June trade with Detroit. The Red Sox sent the Tigers Pesky, Dropo, outfielder Don Lenhardt, third baseman Fred Hatfield, and southpaw Bill Wight in exchange for pitcher Dizzy Trout, outfielder Hoot Evers, shortstop Johnny Lipon, and third baseman George Kell. It was a trade that helped no one, the Tigers sinking to the first last-place finish in their history, while Boston tumbled to sixth.

There were other cast changes in 1952. A burly youngster named Dick Gernert took over at first base, while another talented young performer named Sammy White became the team's regular catcher, a job he called his own for the next eight years.

The most interesting of the new faces, however, and the most exciting and provocative, was a twenty-two-year-old irrepressible named Jimmy Piersall. Piersall came up as a shortstop but was soon switched to the outfield where he was to perform with a brilliance that finally moved Casey Stengel to declare Jimmy among the greatest outfield gloves the old man had ever seen.

Piersall was personable, bright, witty; he could also be caustic, irritating, and offensive, to teammates as well as the opposition. In late May he engaged in a bruising brawl with New York's Billy Martin, and before the day was done got into a punchout with teammate Mickey McDermott.

Most people recognized that Piersall was hyper and tense and quick to explode. Some said he was immature, some attributed his antics to an overly developed competitive zeal. The truth was, Piersall was having a mental breakdown. His outbursts became more explosive, his antics less amusing. One night in June he got on first base and began flapping his arms and yelling "Oink, oink, oink," at the Browns' relief pitcher, Satchel Paige. Piersall's manic performance as he moved from base to base began unnerving the veteran Paige, who finally fed a grand-slam home run to Sammy White as Piersall shrieked with delight. The Browns catcher, Clint Courtney, speaking of Jimmy, remarked after the game, "I believe that man is plumb crazy." The off-the-cuff remark was recalled a month later when Piersall entered a sanitarium. He returned the following season and picked up his career. He played until 1967, and although his behavior was never as aberrant as it had been in the beginning, he was still capable of on-the-field eccentricities that infuriated the opposition and sometimes alienated the fans. Jimmy's story was later told in a book and then in an excellent movie, *Fear*

Strikes Out, with Anthony Perkins giving a superb performance as the tormented young player.

Boudreau brought the team up to fourth place in 1953, the first of four consecutive finishes at the bottom of the first division. Mel Parnell won 21 while McDermott won 18, his most productive year in the majors. Williams returned from the wars for a second time that August, got into 34 games and batted .407. In December 1953 the Sox made one of their better trades, obtaining hard-hitting outfielder Jackie Jensen from Washington for McDermott and outfielder Tom Umphlett.

A gifted athlete, Jensen had been an All-American football player at the University of California. Signed originally by the Yankees, he had been groomed as DiMaggio's successor in center field, but then New York conferred the succession on Mantle and dealt Jensen away. Not only were the Yankees of those years able to dispose of such talent but they were also so abundantly stocked as not to ever miss the man who became the champion RBI hitter of the late 1950s as they took every pennant but two in that decade.

A pull hitter with power, Jensen was one of the few right-handed hitters able to tattoo the left field wall with consistency. Five times in his first six years in Fenway he drove in over 100 runs, leading the league three times. Jackie, however, had a lifelong fear of flying that finally led to his premature retirement in 1959 at the age of thirty-two. He came back two years later, put in a mediocre season, and then quit for good.

In 1954 a bonus baby out of Boston University named Harry Agganis took over at first base for the Red Sox. They called him "the Golden Greek" and he seemed destined for great success. The son of immigrant parents, Agganis had starred in baseball and football at BU, so gifted at the latter sport (he was a quarterback) that he received offers from professional football teams. But baseball was his game, and the Red Sox were his team.

The handsome young man from nearby Lynn apprenticed a year at Louisville and joined the Sox in 1954, fulfilling his lifelong dream. He batted .251, but baseball people liked his swing and the consensus was he would

soon be a .300 hitter. And he started well the following season, batting .313 into the beginning of June, when he had to leave the lineup after being stricken with pneumonia. He was hospitalized and then rejoined the club (prematurely, some people felt; but it was at his own insistence). Soon he was complaining of high fever and chest pains. He was hospitalized again, this time with a severe pulmonary infection complicated by phlebitis. Not long after, on June 27, two months beyond his twenty-fifth birthday, Harry Agganis died of a massive pulmonary embolism—a large blood clot.

Agganis' death had a demoralizing effect on the team and they played lackluster ball that summer, finishing fourth but with a 69–85 record. Boudreau was replaced by former Bosox third baseman Mike (Pinky) Higgins. Higgins ran the club from 1955 till midway through the 1959 season, finishing fourth twice and third twice before giving way to Billy Jurges in 1959. Pinky was the last Red Sox manager to get into the first division until 1967.

Red Sox pitching was just good enough in those years to keep the team finishing third or fourth. A six-foot-seven right-hander named Frank Sullivan tied for the league lead with 18 wins in 1955, while farm products Willard Nixon, Tom Brewer, and Ike Delock seemed to win the same modest quota of games year in and year out.

In 1957 Yawkey startled the baseball world by offering Cleveland a million dollars for their brilliant young left-hander Herb Score, who in two seasons had established himself as perhaps the game's most formidable pitcher. The Indians were no doubt sorely tempted—a million dollars had a much more majestic ring to it in 1957 than it did a quarter-century later, when .280 hitters were demanding it as an annual stipend. The offer, which Cleveland turned down, showed that Yawkey was as determined as ever to bring a winner to Boston. Ironically, a few weeks after refusing the Red Sox offer, the Indians saw Score hit in the eye by a line drive off the bat of New York's Gil McDougald, which virtually ended the young left-hander's career.

So Red Sox fans had to be content with the same show they had been watching since 1939, with time out for one World Series in 1946—

the highly artistic cannonading of American League pitching by Ted Williams. He was getting older, but the news had apparently not yet reached his reflexes. In 1954 he batted .345 but did not qualify for the batting crown because he had only 386 official times at bat, 14 under the requisite number. What made this monstrously unjust was his 136 bases on balls. And so he lost the crown to Cleveland's Bobby Avila, who batted .341. A year later he batted .356 but again did not qualify, Detroit's Al Kaline winning with .340. Because of what happened to Williams, the rules were later changed to allow a man to qualify for the batting crown by number of plate appearances rather than official appearances.

In 1956 Ted batted .345, losing out this time to Mantle's .353. Williams was now thirty-seven years old; but instead of slowing down, he was about to unload his greatest season since 1941, one that is in some respects even greater, taking into account the sixteen added years.

Williams not only took a fifth batting crown in 1957, but he did it with an astonishing .388 batting average, the highest mark since his own landmark .406 figure in 1941. And he did it going away, batting .453 over the second half of the season and over .650 the last ten days.

At the age of thirty-nine he had set a record by becoming the oldest man ever to win a batting championship. A year later he set a new record, winning his sixth and final batting crown at the age of forty. True, this time his numbers were a far less gaudy .328, but they were still the best, edging teammate Pete Runnels by six points. Ted and Pete had been in a virtual tie going into the last few games, but then Williams pulled away with 7-for-11 to take the title. Runnels, an excellent line drive hitter, took the crown the next year with a .320 average and again in 1962 with .326.

Ted Williams retired in 1960 at the age of forty-one, batting .316 in his last year and hitting a home run in his final at bat, circling the bases for the last time to tumultuous cheering from a standing crowd who were applauding not just this home run but all 521 of them, not just this hit but all 2,654 of them. They were cheering his .344 lifetime batting average, the nineteen summers of drama and excitement he

had given them; they were cheering an idol and a legend that had been exclusively theirs. As he ducked into the dugout for the last time—characteristically without tipping his cap—they cheered him on from the contours of old Fenway into the corridors of sports immortals.

Another event in Red Sox history had taken place the year before, in late July. Twelve years after the Brooklyn Dodgers had broken the big league color barrier by bringing up Jackie Robinson, the Red Sox finally integrated their roster, being the last big league club to do so. The player was Elijah (Pumpsie) Green, a twenty-five-year-old infielder.

The history of the Boston Red Sox and black players has been a ticklish one. The club had been coming under increasing criticism from the Boston branch of the National Association for the Advancement of Colored People for what that organization perceived as discrimination. By 1959 Jackie Robinson had been retired for two years, while other black stars like Willie Mays, Henry Aaron, Roberto Clemente, Ernie Banks, Minnie Minoso, Elston Howard, Frank Robinson, etc., had begun to dominate the game.

As far back as 1945, Jackie Robinson and several other blacks had worked out at Fenway, supposedly with an opportunity of signing with the organization. They were rejected. Robinson, never one to mince words, felt it was just showcasing, that the club was never sincere about its interest. Cronin had a different explanation. The then-manager claimed the players were of Triple-A caliber, not yet ready for the majors, and that Boston's only Triple-A club, Louisville, would not, in the prevailing climate, have been the right place to send them. There may have been some rationale in this, but the Red Sox also had a club in Lynn, Massachusetts, in the Class-B New England League, the same league where two young men named Don Newcombe and Roy Campanella played in 1946 with the Dodgers' Nashua, New Hampshire, team.

So it was not until 1959—the year General Manager Joe Cronin left the Red Sox to become American League President—that the first black player joined the Red Sox organization and was promoted to the big team.

The Red Sox got Pinky Higgins from the A's in 1937 and he played for them for two years, batting .302 and .303, before moving on to Detroit. In 1938 Pinky established a major league record by getting 12 consecutive hits, a record tied by Walt Dropo in 1952.

One of the American League's premier busters for many years, Rudy York gave Boston a solid year at first base in 1946 with 17 home runs and 119 runs batted in. He was traded to the White Sox the next year.

100

*Hal Wagner, regular catcher on Boston's 1946
pennant winners. Hal batted .330 in 1944, by
far his best year in the bigs. He was with the
Red Sox from 1944 to 1947.*

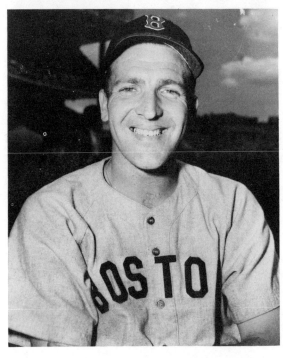

*Joe Dobson pitched for the Red Sox from 1941
through 1950, with a couple of years out for
soldiering. Joe's best year was 1947 when he
was 18–8.*

*Southpaw Mickey
Harris gave the Red
Sox one fine year, in
1946, when he was
17–9.*

101

Johnny Pesky

Sharp-hitting Wally Moses was a twelve-year veteran when the Red Sox picked him up late in the 1946 season. He stayed until 1948.

Power versus power: Feller against Williams.

Left-hander Earl Johnson starred in the Red Sox bullpen in the 1940s. He was 10–4 in 1948.

*Williams batting against the shift in the 1946
World Series at Sportsman's Park, St. Louis.
Note the three infielders on the right side, and
the wide open spaces in the outfield.*

*Dave Ferriss at work against the Cardinals in
the 1946 World Series.*

The date is September 13, 1946, and the Red Sox have just clinched the pennant on Tex Hughson's 1–0 shutout over Cleveland. Boston's lone run came in on Ted Williams' inside-the-park home run. Ted (left) and Hughson.

Bobby Doerr

Ted Williams signing his 1947 contract, on February 3, 1947. With him is the man who originally signed him for the Red Sox, General Manager Eddie Collins. Ted's salary was not revealed, but the guesses ranged from $60,000 to $75,000.

Outfielder Sam Mele joined the Red Sox in 1947 and had a fine rookie year, batting .302. He was traded in 1949, but came back in 1954–55.

Veteran catcher George (Birdie) Tebbetts joined the Red Sox in 1947 and played for them until 1950.

Roy Partee (left) *and Tex Hughson. Partee caught for the Red Sox from 1943 to 1947.*

Rudy York scoring the first run of the 1946 World Series, in the second inning of the opener in St. Louis. Number 8 is Hal Wagner. The Cardinal catcher is Joe Garagiola, the umpire Lee Ballanfant.

Joe McCarthy

The Cardinals' Enos Slaughter being forced at second base by Bobby Doerr who has just fired on to first to double Whitey Kurowski. The action took place in the seventh inning of the third game of the 1946 World Series.

Right-hander Jack Kramer. Jack pitched in Fenway just two years–1948 and 1949. He was 18–5 in '48.

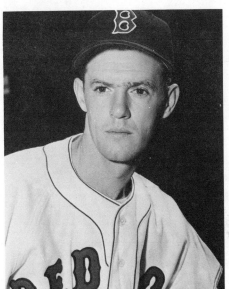

Mickey McDermott, a southpaw with a big league fastball. He joined the Sox in 1948 and pitched for them until 1953, when he was 18–10, his top year.

Vern Stephens. One of the great hitting shortstops of all time, Stephens was ransomed from the Browns in 1948. He had some outstanding seasons in Fenway, including league-leading RBI totals of 159 and 144 in 1949–50. He was traded to the White Sox in 1953.

Ellis Kinder, acquired from the Browns after the 1947 season. Kinder pitched for the Red Sox until 1955. His best year was 1949 when he was 23–6.

Al Zarilla was with the Red Sox in 1949 and 1950, then was traded to Chicago. He hit .325 in 1950.

Right-hander Denny Galehouse. Denny was originally with the Red Sox in 1939–40, was traded to the Browns, and then reacquired in 1947. He was released in 1949.

Chuck Stobbs, shown here when he was with the Washington Senators, came up with the Red Sox in 1947 and stayed until 1951. He was 11–6 in 1949, 12–7 a year later.

Mel Parnell, one of Boston's all-time left-handers. He spent his entire ten-year big league career with the Red Sox, from 1947 through 1956. His top years were 1949 (25–7) and 1953 (21–8). Lifetime he was 123–75.

Billy Goodman, perhaps the best of all utility men. He played first, second, third, and the outfield with equal proficiency. He was with the Red Sox from 1947 to 1957. In his nine full seasons he never batted under .293. He won the batting championship in 1950 with .354.

Outfielder Stan Spence came up with the Red Sox in 1940, was traded to Washington in 1942, and came back to Boston in 1948.

Son of Hall of Famer George Sisler, Dave Sisler pitched for the Red Sox from 1956 to 1959.

112

Outfielder Clyde Vollmer played for the Red Sox from 1950 to 1953. His career was unexceptional—except for the month of July in 1951 when he hit 13 homers and came through with a dazzling string of clutch, game-winning hits. After that, it was back to the placid life of a journeyman .250 hitter.

Matt Batts, Red Sox catcher from 1947 to 1951. He hit .314 as a part-timer in 1948.

Thunder over Boston. Left to right: *Williams, Stephens, and Dropo in June 1950.
Even with Ted missing half the season, they drove in 385 runs between them that year.*

*Manager and future
manager: Steve
O'Neill (left) and Lou
Boudreau at Sarasota
in March 1951.*

ht-hander Willard
on pitched for
ton from 1950 to
8. Twelve wins in
and '57 was the
st he could muster.

First baseman Dick
Gernert was with the
Red Sox from 1952
through 1959. He had
21 home runs in 1953,
his top figure.

It's July 14, 1956, and Mel Parnell has just pitched a no-hitter against the White Sox. With him is catcher Sammy White.

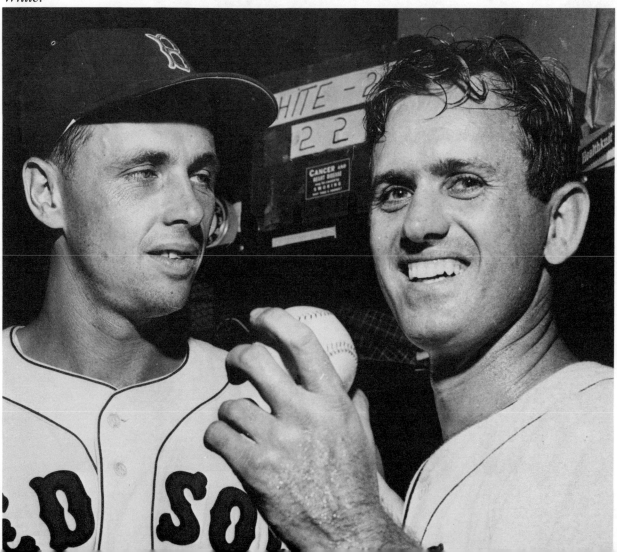

One of the great third baseman of all time, George Kell was acquired from the Tigers in June 1952. He batted .311 that year, .307 the next, then was traded to the White Sox in 1954.

The eyes of a .400 hitter. Williams in the middle 1950s.

Trying to bolster their pitching, the Red Sox acquired Bill Wight (left) and Ray Scarborough from the White Sox in 1951. By the end of 1952 both were gone.

Infielder Ted Lepcio was with the Red Sox from 1952 to 1959.

Below: Bill Henry, left-handed relief pitcher with the team from 1952 to 1955.

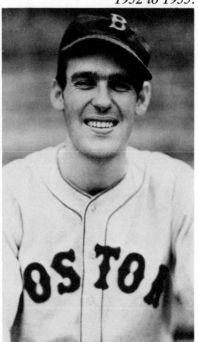

Jimmy Piersall dazzled, entertained, and occasionally infuriated them in the Red Sox outfield from 1950 through 1958. Jimmy's highwater mark in Boston was .293 in 1956. He was traded to Cleveland in 1959.

Milt Bolling, Red Sox shortstop from 1952 to 1957. His best was .263 in 1953.

118

Gene Stephens, reserve outfielder from 1952 to 1960.

Jackie Jensen

119

Getting loose.

Ivan (Ike) Delock, who pitched for Boston from 1952 to 1963. The right-hander's best year was 1958 when he was 14–8.

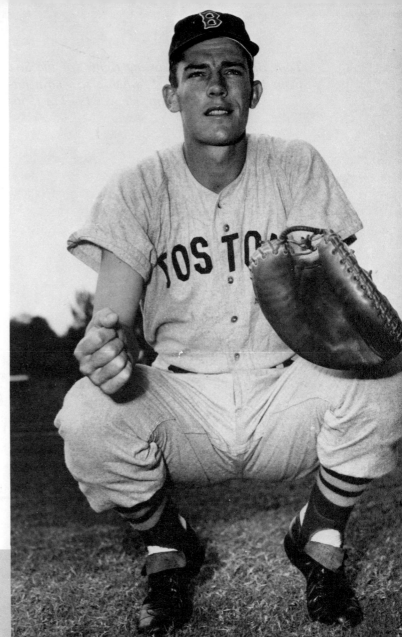

Haywood Sullivan: from .150 hitter to club owner.

Frank Sullivan, Red Sox right-hander from 1953 through 1960. Frank's best year was 1955 when he won 18, good enough to tie for the league lead that year.

Tom Brewer, hard-throwing righty for the Sox from 1954 through 1961, when a sore arm finished him. He was 19–9 in 1956.

Harry Agganis

The Red Sox acquired Mike Fornieles from Baltimore in 1957 and he became a fine relief pitcher for them, leading the league with 70 appearances in 1960. He pitched for Boston until 1963.

Billy Klaus played in the Red Sox infield from 1955 to 1958. He batted .283 in 1955, his highest mark.

123

The 1958 season has just ended on September 28 and Ted Williams has won his sixth batting title, edging out teammate Pete Runnels by six points, .328. to .322. Williams (left) and Runnels.

Left: Norm Zauchin, a big first baseman, broke in with the Sox in 1951, then came back in 1955 and clubbed 27 homers. He never repeated that performance, however, and by 1958 was gone.

Right: Don Buddin, Red Sox shortstop from 1956 to 1961.

Former Yankee fast-baller Bob Porterfield, a Red Sox pitcher in 1955 and 1956.

Below: Leo Kiley came up to the big team from out of the farm system in 1951 and remained until 1959, pitching mostly in relief.

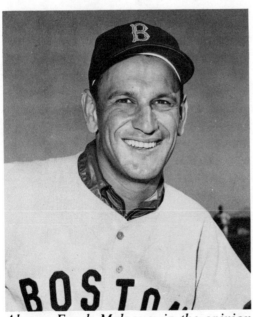

Above: Frank Malzone, in the opinion of many the greatest of all Red Sox third basemen. He covered the bag for Boston from 1955 through 1965. His top year was .295 in 1958.

A bonus pitcher who joined the Sox in 1955, Frank Baumann was with them until 1959.

Williams during the 1958 season.

Pumpsie Green, Boston's first black player. He played with the club from 1959 through 1962.

The twenty-two-year veteran in his final season, 1960.

127

7 · YAZ AND THE IMPOSSIBLE DREAM

WHEN THE 1961 SEASON OPENED, Williams was gone. Usually the departure of a player of superstar magnitude, like Williams, leaves behind a void that can take decades to fill. There have been a few, rare, exceptions to this rule of probability. Ruth left the Yankees in 1934; DiMaggio joined the club in 1936. In 1951 DiMaggio retired; it was the same year Mantle became a Yankee. Boston's contribution to the lore of superstar decline and replacement occurred in 1961 when Williams' place in left field was taken by a twenty-one-year-old native of eastern Long Island named Carl Yastrzemski.

When he was a sophomore at Notre Dame, Yastrzemski's smooth left-handed swing had done enough damage to attract a $40,000 bonus offer from the Yankees. But the young man's father was insisting on $100,000. The Red Sox accepted Mr. Yastrzemski's evaluation and cut a check in that amount. Dispatched to Raleigh in the Carolina League in 1959, the youngster handed his employers the first dividend on their investment with a .377 batting average. A year later, playing in fast company with Minneapolis of the American Association, Yaz batted .339. The following spring he was standing in the awesome shadow of the departed Williams, heralded as the replacement for the irreplaceable.

He started slowly with a .266 batting average for his first season, a season that saw him receive some midsummer tutoring from Williams. The great slugger never for a moment doubted Yastrzemski's talent. The young man reminded him of himself, Williams said. Yaz had the ability, the stroke, the intensity, the highly charged desire to attack a pitched ball.

"He positively *quivered* waiting for that next pitch," Williams said.

Yastrzemski's talent was not limited to swinging the bat. He had no peer as a defensive outfielder, nor was there a better throwing arm in baseball. Like DiMaggio, Mays, and Clemente, he was a fearsome all-around threat on a ball field.

If Yastrzemski had a problem, it was occasionally with his attitude. Surrounded by inept ball clubs his first six years in the majors (the highest the Red Sox finished from 1961 through 1966 was sixth), he could become moody, leading to accusations of not expending his greatest effort. Billy Herman, who managed the Red Sox in 1965 and 1966, recalled his brooding star vividly.

"How did I get along Yastrzemski?" Herman said in response to a question. "Like everybody else did. By that I mean nobody ever got along with Yastrzemski. Every manager has trouble with him, and some of them had it by the ton. He plays only as hard as he wants to play, and any manager is going to resent that, I don't give a damn who it is, because his job depends upon the players producing.

"What gets you so mad is that the guy has as much ability as anybody in the game. If he gave you a hundred percent every time he walked out on the field, if he had the attitude of, say, a Pete Reiser or an Enos Slaughter or a Pete Rose, you'd never hear about another player, he'd be so outstanding."

The Red Sox languished in the second division for eight straight years, beginning in 1959, their most arid spell since the 1920s. Higgins was followed as manager by former National

League shortstop Billy Jurges. After Jurges was let out in 1960, Higgins came back. In 1962 former Red Sox hero Johnny Pesky replaced Higgins and in turn gave way to Herman two years later.

Those were bleak years for the Red Sox, stretching even the loyalty of their fans. In 1965 attendance dropped to 650,000, lowest in twenty years. Now and then there were some individual achievements to cheer about, like Yastrzemski's first batting title in 1963 (.321). In 1961 right-handers Earl Wilson (the club's second black player) and Bill Monbouquette, two men who gave the pitching staff a semblance of respectability in those years, each pitched a no-hitter. In 1963 "Mombo" was 20–10, the first Red Sox pitcher since Parnell in 1953 to win 20.

In 1962 a right-handed relief pitcher named Dick Radatz appeared on the scene and immediately became the most intimidating bullpen operative in the league. Nicknamed "The Monster" because of his six-foot-six-inch 230-pound frame, Radatz was for three years nearly unhittable. From 1962 through 1964 he won 40 games and saved 78 others. Through that span he pitched 413 innings, gave up just 292 hits, and struck out 487, most of them with a blazing fastball he served up with a seemingly effortless sidearm motion. The big man slumped off after the 1964 season and early in '66 was traded to Cleveland, never to regain his early form.

In 1963 the Red Sox had another RBI leader in first baseman Dick Stuart, who hit 42 home runs and drove in 118 runs. The only question was whether Stuart was letting in more runs with his glove than he was sending across with his bat. Nicknamed "Dr. Strangeglove" by the press, he was called "a menace" in the field by Manager Pesky. After another big RBI Year in 1964—114—Stuart packed his big bat and hapless glove and moved on to Philadelphia.

In 1964 the Sox unveiled an exciting young outfielder named Tony Conigliaro. Tony C. became an instant hero when he shelled one over the wall in his Fenway debut. The nineteen-year-old youngster from nearby Swampscott hit 24 bombs in his rookie year and came

back in 1965 to become the youngest home run champ ever, with a total of 32. He hit 28 the next year and it seemed that one of the great careers in Red Sox history was in the making.

In 1966 the Sox finished ninth for the second year in a row. (The only solace for Red Sox fans that year was the Yankees finishing tenth.) Predictably, Billy Herman was let out as manager. The new man was a thirty-six-year-old former journeyman ballplayer named Dick Williams.

Williams, whose major league career had ended with the Red Sox in 1964, had been grooming himself for a managerial career for years. Sharp-eyed, curious, observant, he possessed one of the game's keener minds. Proud of the fact that he had been influenced by Charlie Dressen (for whom he had played in Brooklyn), Bobby Bragan, and Paul Richards, Williams was a firm believer in his players knowing how to execute the fundamentals—the cut-off, the run-down, the relay, etc.

Also part of Williams' makeup was a sometimes caustic tongue that could be turned on anyone from umpires to opponents to his own players, a drill instructor's relentless insistence upon things being done his way, and a zealous desire to win.

"Mental mistakes I can't tolerate," he said. "A man has to know what he's got to do on the field at all times, and it's got to be automatic. Missing a cut-off man looks like a physical action; to me it's a mental mistake. It shouldn't happen. I can't tolerate a guy missing signs. I won't tolerate it. And I tell these guys that. There's no excuse for missing a sign."

Beginning with spring training in 1967, he brought his uncompromising drive to the Red Sox and never let up. He drove his players hard, he harangued them, goaded them, insisting they could win it all and never mind the ninth-place finish of a year before.

"The players probably thought I was crazy as a loon," he said. "But, hell, I had a one-year contract. So if I was crazy, I was going to be crazy all year and give it the best I had. Frankly, I didn't make too many friends among the players that year . . . I don't care if they like me or not. I am concerned, though, about them respecting my knowledge of the game. If they do, they'll play for me, and they'll play at the top of their ability."

And so they did, giving Boston fans what is probably still the most thrilling year in all Red Sox history, driving up from ninth place to capture the pennant on the last day of the season.

THE IMPOSSIBLE DREAM

The team that Williams drove to the pennant averaged twenty-five years of age, youngest in the league. Yastrzemski at twenty-seven was now the veteran among the regulars. At first base was George Scott, a power hitter with a magic glove. Rookie Mike Andrews was at second. Rico Petrocelli was at shortstop and Joe Foy at third. Yastrzemski, COnigliaro, and talented rookie Reggie Smith were in the outfield. The catching was shared by Mike Ryan, Russ Gibson, and a late-season acquisition from the Yankees, Elston Howard.

The pitching was headed by Jim Lonborg, a tall right-hander who was 22–9 and led the league in strikeouts with 246. Behind him were righties José Santiago (12–4) and Gary Bell (12–8), and a strong relief pitcher, burly right-hander John Wyatt.

Not a very prepossessing team. Not nearly as strong as many Red Sox teams that did not win pennants. But they were galvanized all season long by Williams, who came to Fenway, looked at The Wall, and devised a strategy.

"I made up my mind when I took over the Red Sox," he said, "that the left field wall was not going to be a factor in the way I ran the game. I'd played there in '63 and '64 and saw too many good hitters ruining themselves taking shots at that wall. I didn't want that to happen with my club. We didn't gear ourselves to try to hit the wall. We bunted, we squeezed, we hit to the right side to move a guy from second to third, we stole, and we hit-and-run. We didn't lay back and wait for the big inning.

"As far as our pitching was concerned, we pitched in on the right-handed hitters. They always came up there looking for the ball away, figuring we'd try to keep them from pulling.

But I think the way to pitch in Fenway Park is inside. Keep doing that and gradually you'll back them up a little—then go outside with it, and it'll be very effective. Jim Lonborg did that beautifully for us all year; so did José Santiago."

They won the pennant despite a shocking injury to their young star, Tony Conigliaro. On August 18, Conigliaro was struck on the left side of the face by a fastball fired by Jack Hamilton. The force of the blow fractured Tony's cheekbone, dislocated his jaw, and damaged the retina in his left eye. Over the next few years he made several game attempts to come back, but he was never the same player.

The catalyst for the Red Sox in the year of "The Impossible Dream" was Yastrzemski. Yaz had a year of which legends are carved. He batted .326 to lead the league, drove in 121 runs to lead the league, and earned a Triple Crown when his 44 home runs tied Minnesota's Harmon Killebrew for the top spot. But it wasn't just his statistics that earned Yastrzemski a New England halo in 1967, it was how and when he accumulated them.

Playing with the full fury of the greatness that had been predicted for him, playing for the first time with a World Series goal in front of him, Yaz hit consistently, and dramatically, in the clutch. Coming into the final few games of the season, four clubs had a shot at it—the Red Sox, Twins, White Sox, and Tigers. The White Sox were the first to be eliminated. In the final two games of the season the Red Sox eliminated the Twins. On the last day, after their victory, they listened on the radio as the Tigers lost to the Angels, thus preventing a Boston-Detroit tie and giving the Red Sox their first pennant in twenty-one years.

Playing under mounting pressure, Yastrzemski connected for 23 hits in his last 44 at bats, including 10 for his last 13, 7 for his last 8, and 4-for-4 on the final day. In other words, as things got tougher, he got better.

As it had been in 1946, so it was in 1967— the Red Sox versus the Cardinals. There were two other parallels: the Cards won in seven, and one of their pitchers won three games.

The emotionally drained Sox put up a stubborn fight, but they ran square into a buzzsaw named Bob Gibson, one of baseball's greatest pitchers. Gibson beat them in Game One, 2–1; shut them out 6–0 in Game Four, and whipped them again in the finale, 7–2. In hurling three complete-game victories, the Cardinal fastballer fanned 26 in 27 innings and posted an ERA of 1.00.

For Boston, it was as it had been all season—Yastrzemski and Lonborg. Yaz never stopped hitting—.400 in the Series, including 3 home runs. Lonborg pitched a 1-hit shutout in Game Two and a 3-hit victory in Game Five. But Big Jim, coming back on two days' rest in Game Seven, finally ran out of gas.

A 100-to-1 shot in spring training, a pennant on the last day, a seven-game World Series— the Red Sox left behind an excitement that warmed the towns and cities of New England through the long, snow-piled winter.

The 1967 pennant had been so unexpected, so pulse-beating, so exquisitely storybook, there was almost no way it could happen again. Nor did it. In fact, the dream began evaporating that winter. At the end of December Lonborg tore up the ligaments in his left knee in a skiing accident at Lake Tahoe. The big right-hander was never the same. He pitched four more years for Boston, compiling a 27–29 record before being traded to Milwaukee.

Yastrzemski dropped to .301, which was good enough to lead the league in that "Year of the Pitcher." George Scott dropped to an anemic .171, Petrocelli batted .234, Foy .225, and so it went. Ken Harrelson, signed as a free agent the year before after having been dropped by Kansas City, made the most noise in the Boston lineup, hitting 35 home runs and leading the league with 109 runs batted in.

The team finished fourth in 1968 and third the next year. By the end of the '69 season miracle manager Williams was gone. When asked why he thought he had been fired, Williams said, "I heard that Tom Yawkey said I was too tough on the players. Maybe so, but I was also pretty tough on the turnstiles too— the Red Sox had three of the biggest attendance years in their history the three years I was there."

Williams was followed by Eddie Kasko, who ran the club for four years, earning two third-place finishes and two seconds.

In late March 1972 those historically minded Red Sox fans still haunted by the ghosts of past mistakes winced painfully: the Red Sox and the Yankees had just completed a deal. Having dealt George Scott to Milwaukee, the Sox were in need of a first baseman. The man they coveted was New York's Danny Cater. He was the man they got. In exchange they sent the Yankees twenty-six-year-old southpaw reliever Albert (Sparky) Lyle, possessor of a tireless left arm that threw one of the most wicked sliders in the league. Sparky promptly became one of the finest relief pitchers in baseball, while Cater put in three forgettable seasons in Boston and then faded away. (What the Red Sox seem to need is legislation forbidding dealing with the Yankees.)

The year that began with the Sparky Lyle trade ended with the Red Sox losing the division title by a half-game to Detroit. (With expansion had come divisional play, beginning in 1969.) Going into Detroit for their final three games of the season, the Sox held a half-game lead. The Tigers tipped them over by a 4–1 score in the opener, a game marked by a baserunning snafu committed by one of the game's most adept baserunners, thirty-eight-year-old Luis Aparicio, acquired by Boston from the White Sox two years before. Aparicio took a tumble rounding third base that broke the back of a Red Sox rally, after which they never really threatened again. The Tigers polished them off the next day to clinch the division.

The '72 Red Sox did come away from that disappointing season with one or two positive signs for the future. One was provided by their husky, ruggedly good-looking rookie catcher, Carlton Fisk. Not only did Fisk (known as "Pudge") hit .293 with 22 home runs, but he also gave the team some solid leadership behind the plate. The rookie took charge of the pitching staff and was not above walking out to the mound and berating his pitchers if he thought they were becoming a bit lax in their efforts. Nor was he intimidated by his veteran teammates. In August, in the heat of the pennant race, he reportedly accused Yastrzemski and Reggie Smith of going at less than full throttle. According to a Massachusetts paper, Fisk said that the two "are not lending inspiration to the team and their attitude is a big disappointment." Carlton Fisk had come to town.

Another signpost pointing to the future was named Luis Tiant. After some brilliant seasons with Cleveland, the Cuban right-hander had lost his stuff and been sent to the minors, from where the Red Sox picked him up. After a 1–7 record in 1971, Luis began in 1972 a string of winning seasons during which he became one of the most popular players ever to wear a Red Sox uniform. With an ingratiating personality, a colorful whirl-around style on the mound, and a big trademark cigar clenched between an engaging smile, Luis won the hearts of Fenway fans, beginning with his 15–6 record and league-leading 1.91 ERA in 1972.

With a new manager, Darrell Johnson, at the helm in 1974, the club finished third, 7 games behind the Orioles. But now the pump was being primed. The farm system had coughed up a veritable galaxy of glittering young players. Cecil Cooper shared first base with Yastrzemski. Rick Burleson, an aggressive hard-nosed performer, was moving in at shortstop. Dwight Evans, a youngster with a howitzer arm, was now in right field. And at the end of the season a couple of outfielders named Fred Lynn and Jim Rice joined the club. It was as impressive an influx of bright young talent as any club had enjoyed in years.

With the powerhouse Orioles and rejuvenated Yankees in the East Division, the Red Sox were not widely picked to win in 1975. The prophets may be forgiven, however, for no one could have foreseen what rookies Lynn and Rice were about to unleash upon the league.

Red Sox fans would have to go back to Jimmie Foxx before finding a right-handed batter with the power that Jim Rice had. He hit 22 home runs, drove in 102 runs, and batted .309. Lynn did even better. On his way to an unprecedented sweep of both Most Valuable Player and Rookie of the Year honors, Lynn batted .331, hit 21 homers, drove in 105 runs, led with a .566 slugging mark and 47 doubles, in addition to playing a superb center field. The Rice-Lynn-Evans outfield was the greatest

Boston had seen since the days of Hooper-Speaker-Lewis.

With Fisk batting .331 (despite losing a half season to injuries), second base pick-up Denny Doyle .310, and first baseman–designated hitter Cecil Cooper at .311, the Sox had five .300 hitters in the lineup. With Yastrzemski at first, Burleson at short, and veteran Rico Petrocelli at third, the Sox were well covered at every outpost. On the bench was outfielder Bernie Carbo, hitting solidly when he could get in a game.

Johnson's pitching staff was led by right-hander Rick Wise (19–12), Tiant (18–14), and left-hander Bill Lee (17–9). Lee was dubbed "Spaceman" for the witty, sometimes abstruse abstractions he uttered, as well as for the generally unconventional approach he took to life. Behind his front three, Johnson had lefty Roger Moret (14–3) and righty Reggie Cleveland (13–9). In the bullpen the noblest work was done by speedballer Dick Drago, who notched 15 saves. It was a rare instance in Red Sox history when strong pitching matched the club's heavy hitting.

Winning by 4½ over Baltimore, the Sox kept going and swept three-time world champions Oakland in the championship series. With Rice sidelined by a September hand injury, Yastrzemski took over in left field. With the scent of pennant blood once more in his nostrils, the thirty-five-year-old veteran took a draught of 1967 elixir and led the club with a .455 average, playing left field with such patented splendor that an awed Reggie Jackson (then with Oakland) said later, "From now on I'm calling him Mister."

WAITING FOR THE RED SOX

Waiting for the Red Sox in the World Series was one of the greatest teams in baseball history—the Cincinnati Reds, the relentless "Big Red Machine." The primary gears in this steamroller were named Pete Rose, Johnny Bench, Joe Morgan, George Foster, Tony Perez, Dave Concepcion, Ken Griffey. The pitchers were Don Gullett, Gary Nolan, and

Jack Billingham, backed up by a remarkably deep relief corps consisting of Pedro Borbon, Clay Carroll, Will McEnaney, and Rawley Eastwick. This ball club had torn the National League apart, winning their division title by 20 games over the Dodgers and then sweeping Pittsburgh three straight in the championship series.

Because of the quality of talent on both sides, it looked like an exciting Series. It was that, and more. It has been called "The Greatest Series Ever," with a sixth game that featured the defensive brilliance and the sudden explosiveness that makes baseball the most rewarding of all spectator sports.

Tiant got the Sox off to a fast start when he shut the Reds out at Fenway by a score of 6–0, Boston scoring all of its runs in the last of the seventh. Bill Lee carried a 2–1 lead into the top of the ninth of Game Two, only to see Cincinnati score twice and sneak off with a 3–2 win, tying the Series.

The two clubs then flew to Cincinnati. There, the Reds took two out of three and returned to Boston needing just one more win to clinch the title.

Game Six of the 1975 World Series remains the game that future World Series thrillers will be measured against. It was Tiant against Gary Nolan, but by the time it was over, four hours later, Cincinnati skipper Sparky Anderson had used eight pitchers and Darrell Johnson four. Fred Lynn sent Boston hopes skyrocketing with a 3-run bomb in the first inning. But by the last of the eighth the Reds had built up a 6–3 lead and Red Sox hopes were traveling on empty. But then two men were on base and Johnson sent up a former Cincinnati player Bernie Carbo to pinch-hit. Used sparingly, Carbo had pinch-hit a home run earlier in the Series. And suddenly he shocked Fenway Park as well as taverns and living rooms up and down New England and all across America when he did it again, sending the ball far out into the night, tying the game at 6–6.

In the bottom of the ninth the Sox loaded the bases with none out, only to allow the Reds wriggle off the hook when George Foster took Lynn's fly ball along the left field line and threw Denny Doyle out at the plate.

In the top of the eleventh it was Dwight Evans' turn to uncork a miracle. With one out and Ken Griffey on first, Joe Morgan ripped one toward the right field seats. It had, as the cliche goes, home run written all over it. But Evans ran back and made a spectacular grab of the ball just before it got into the seats. He then turned injury into insult by firing into the infield and doubling up Griffey.

The game rolled on to the bottom of the twelfth inning. Playing extra innings in Fenway is like dropping lighted matches near a powder keg—before long there is going to be a big noise. And so it happened. The first man up was Carlton Fisk. He wasted no time, lofting right-hander Pat Darcy's first pitch high along the left field line. There was no question about distance, only whether it was fair or foul. Fisk stood at home plate pushing his arms through the air toward fair territory, trying to guide the ball. He succeeded. The ball struck the foul pole and an appreciative Fisk began to applaud. Fenway erupted to the skies as Fisk began running out what is probably the most memorable home run in Red Sox history.

Almost inevitably, the seventh game was decided by one run, and almost inevitably, it was scored in the ninth inning, as if destiny could not make up its mind which of these two finely balanced ball clubs should be crowned champion and waited until the last possible moment before filing a decision.

After taking a 3–0 lead in the bottom of the third, the Red Sox watched the Reds begin nipping at it, scoring two in the top of the sixth, the tying run in the top of the seventh, and the game-winner in the top of the ninth. The championship run scored on a soft single dropped into short center by Joe Morgan, and for the third time since Tom Yawkey had bought the team the Red Sox had fallen short in a seven-game Series.

The Sox failed to repeat in 1976, but it wasn't because Yawkey was not trying. In the middle of June word passed that a financially ailing Charlie Finley was willing to break up his Oakland club for some ready cash. The Yankees quickly purchased left-handed ace Vida Blue for around a million dollars, while the Red Sox shelled out a million apiece for left-fielder Joe Rudi and relief pitcher Rollie Fingers. Where Boston would have played Rudi was not clear, for not even this splendid ballplayer could have squeezed into the Rice-Lynn-Evans combine. It all became academic, however, when Commissioner Bowie Kuhn voided the sales as being detrimental to the game's best interests. It was widely suspected at the time that Kuhn was trying to put the kibosh on Finley, his most bitter antagonist among the club owners. Finley filed a $10-million lawsuit against Kuhn, but the courts eventually upheld the commissioner.

The buzz of the aborted sale had just about quieted down when on July 9 leukemia ended the life of Tom Yawkey. Few people had known the Red Sox owner was seriously ill. Tom Yawkey's death bespoke his life—quiet and without fanfare.

After forty-four years, the man who had taken the moribund Red Sox franchise and built it into a New England institution was gone. Fittingly for a man who had seen his Grove and his Foxx and his Williams and his Yastrzemski set records, Yawkey had himself set a couple. He had operated a major league team longer than anyone else. And it had been said of Tom Yawkey that he was often too generous with his players, that he cared too much about them. The first record may some day conceivably be broken. The second seems secure.

The Sox finished third in 1976, 15½ behind the Yankees. Along the way Darrell Johnson learned just how tenuous is the job of a big league manager. The man who had won the pennant less than a year before was suddenly canned and replaced by one of his coaches, Don Zimmer.

Several months after the end of the 1976 season, the Red Sox made a disastrous trade. They sent Cecil Cooper to Milwaukee in exchange for their former first baseman George Scott. The "Boomer" had one decent year for Boston and then faded out; Cooper went on to become one of the league's most lethal hitters for Milwaukee.

In 1977 Zimmer brought the club home to a second-place tie with Baltimore, 2½ games be-

hind the Yankees. The club's 97 victories were the most since the 1946 pennant winner took 104. The team looked like a Red Sox outfit of old—heavy hitting and thin pitching. They orbited 213 home runs, fourth highest total in American League history, and batted .281. Jim Rice led the club and league with 39, followed by Scott's 33, Butch Hobson's 30, Yastrzemski's 28, and Fisk's 26. Hobson, Yaz, Fisk, and Rice all drove in over 100 runs. But the top winner on the mound was free agent signee Bill Campbell with just 13, all of them chalked up via the bullpen.

The 1978 Red Sox were even stronger, a team that could not lose. The club had strengthened itself considerably via trades and the free agent signing of right-hander Mike Torrez, a Yankee ace the year before. They also bolstered the pitching staff by mesmerizing the Indians out of right-hander Dennis Eckersley during spring training. To get "The Eck," Boston swapped Rick Wise and several lesser lights. Another excellent addition was second baseman Jerry Remy, acquiring him from California for young right-hander Don Aase.

Behind the explosive bat of Jim Rice, who put together one of the greatest slugging seasons in decades, and the strong pitching of Eckersley, Torrez, Tiant, and reliever Bob Stanley, the Red Sox tore apart the league the first half of the season. In mid-July they held a 10-game lead over second-place Milwaukee. They were 14 games ahead of an injury-riddled, dissension-torn Yankee club in fourth.

The Sox were doing it all under new ownership. In May a group headed by Yawkey's widow Jean, Buddy LeRoux, and Haywood Sullivan had acquired the team for around $15 million. Mrs. Yawkey was installed as club president; LeRoux, formerly the team's trainer, was in charge of the business and administration portfolios; while Sullivan took over player personnel. Sullivan was an interesting story. He had been signed as a catcher by the Sox in 1952 for a large bonus, estimated as high as $95,000. He never panned out as a player, getting into just 60 games for Boston over four years and batting .150. In the middle

1960s he joined the club's front office as vice-president in charge of player personnel, working under General Manager Dick O'Connell, with whom he later contested for club ownership. So Sullivan rose from .150 hitter to club owner, the moral of which is best left to the sages to ponder.

COLLAPSE

The world began to tilt under the Red Sox in mid-July. The Yankee injured began to heal and return to the lineup. The contentious Billy Martin was replaced by a placid, soothing Bob Lemon. As the Red Sox stumbled, Yankee victories began hitting the scoreboard with machine-gun regularity. A slender lefty named Ron Guidry put together a 25–3 season, a moody righty named Ed Figueroa was 20–9, a sore-armed Catfish Hunter made a miraculous late-season recovery, and a dynamic bullpen duo of Goose Gossage and ex-Red Soxer Sparky Lyle made sure no late-inning advantage was dissipated.

Altogether, the Yankees won 52 of their last 73, making one of the most remarkable drives in baseball history. For Boston, the key tumble came between August 30 and September 16 when the club lost 14 of 17. It was during this stretch that the Red Sox suffered through one of the most horrendous four-day episodes imaginable. The Yankees came to town trailing by 4, with 4 to play. The Red Sox proved to be the most hospitable of hosts. The scores were 15–3, 13–2, 7–0, and 7–4, and the Yankees (probably to their own astonishment as much as anyone else's) left town in a tie for first.

Manager Don Zimmer was gradually becoming a very unpopular man in Boston. Not only was the skipper being roasted nightly on the town's many sports talk shows, but he was also hearing some unflattering comments coming out of his own clubhouse. Left-hander Bill Lee called the manager the team's "designated gerbil," while others were questioning Zim's judgment in various matters. Lee, with a lease on the manager's doghouse, hardly pitched at all during the final five weeks; Zimmer even went

so far as to start a pea-green rookie southpaw named Bobby Sprowl in one of the key games against the Yankees, with predictable results.

Zimmer pulled his men together for a strong stretch run, winning eleven of the last thirteen, including the final seven in a row, earning a tie with the Yankees.

The playoff for the eastern division title took place on a bright autumn afternoon in Fenway. The match-up was Torrez versus Guidry, not a very promising one for Boston since Torrez had hardly won anything over the past month and Guidry had hardly lost anything all year. But Big Mike, putting his heart into every pitch, held the Yankees to just two hits over the first six innings, while his mates were squeezing two runs out of Guidry, one of them on a Yastrzemski home run that barely wrapped itself around the foul pole.

Then came the top of the seventh. Singles by Chris Chambliss and Roy White, and Bucky Dent coming up, carrying the lightest bat of any Yankee regular. A .240 hitter with just 4 homers all season. Not the kind of fellow you'd expect to spoil your afternoon, much less your entire year.

A soft, high fly ball out toward left field. Torrez said later he didn't think it would carry. Yastrzemski looked as though he might have a play on it. But he didn't. The ball had just enough pulse in it to putter through the air and drop into the screen for a 3-run homer.

For fans with a sense of history, it was the second time that a light-hitting Yankee infielder had rapped the clutch 3-run hit—in 1949 it had been Jerry Coleman's base-clearing rap that broke the Red Sox' heart (as well as other parts of the anatomy). Like Coleman's, Dent's blow was less than resounding coming off the bat; but when it landed it made the cash registers ring.

The Yankees scored another run in that inning, and another in the top of the eighth—a home run by Reggie Jackson, the actual game-winner (a fact generally overlooked, except perhaps by Reggie).

The Red Sox had some kick left. They pushed the score up to 5–4 and had the tying run at third with 2 out in the last of the ninth, with Yastrzemski at bat. By now it was Gossage on the mound, throwing fastballs far beyond the legal speed limit. With the count 1–0, Yaz turned Boston into a modern-day counterpart of old Mudville when he popped one up to third baseman Graig Nettles who took it in foul ground. And that was that. Zimmer's club had won 99 games, fourth highest total in Red Sox history, more than forty-five previous American League pennant winners—and still no cigar.

There were some consolations. Jim Rice edged Guidry for MVP honors. The Red Sox left fielder hit with devastating authority all season, leading with 46 home runs, 15 triples, 213 hits, 139 runs batted in, .600 slugging average, 406 total bases. The latter figure was notable—Rice was the first American Leaguer since DiMaggio in 1937 to pile up 400 total bases. Eckersley was a 20-game winner and Bob Stanley emerged as a bullpen ace with a 15–2 record.

In 1979 the Red Sox finished ahead of the Yankees. The catch was, the Yankees finished fourth, Boston third. The Sox had allowed Luis Tiant to become a free agent and the portly veteran, a long-time Fenway favorite, was signed by the Yankees to a two-year contract. Fred Lynn won the batting crown with a .333 average, mid-season pick-up Bob Watson (from Houston) hit .337, Rice .325. Rice and Lynn each clubbed 39 homers and drove in 130 and 122 runs respectively. But it wasn't enough.

In 1980 the team finished fourth in an injury-plagued season. At one time or another, Eckersley, Lynn, Rice, Hobson, and Remy were shelved. The Red Sox also found themselves facing another problem—they happened to be in baseball's strongest division, competing with New York, Baltimore, and Milwaukee. The Yankees had a well-balanced team, plus George Steinbrenner's relentless pursuit of free agents; Baltimore was always a contender, thanks to strong pitching and a productive farm system; and Milwaukee had developed into an awesome power plant (thanks in part to ex-Boston players Cecil Cooper and Ben Oglivie).

The 1980 season closed with the dismissal of Don Zimmer. The little round man had done well in his four Fenway years, winning 411 and losing 304, but he hadn't won the big one in 1978 and had no pennants to show for his tenure. In addition, the Fenway crowd had taken a dislike to him, and justly or unjustly, nothing will tie the can more quickly to a manager than fan disapproval.

Replacing Zimmer was Ralph Houk, former skipper of the Yankees and Tigers, whom the club lured out of retirement. Rugged, a former war hero (he had served as a major in the Rangers in World War II), and an incurable optimist, Houk had always been known as a players' manager. He defended them, fought for them, backed them to the hilt.

The major would need all the optimism he could muster as he prepared to face the 1981 season. Rick Burleson, linchpin of the infield, and Fred Lynn each had one year left on their contracts. Each would be asking for more money than the Red Sox cared to pay. In December, Burleson and Butch Hobson were traded to California for relief pitcher Mark Clear, third baseman Carney Lansford, and outfielder Rick Miller, back for a second hitch in Fenway. It turned out to be an excellent trade for Boston, unfortunate for California when Burleson suffered a serious shoulder injury after one year in California. Lansford won a batting title in the strike-aborted 1981 season, while Clear gave the Sox strong relief work, and Miller played well in center field.

A month later, Lynn was swapped to California with pitcher Steve Renko for lefty Frank Tanana, outfielder Joe Rudi, and a minor leaguer. That swap was all California as neither Tanana nor Rudi performed up to past glory.

A clerical foul-up also cost Boston Carlton Fisk. Because Fisk's contract had been mailed too late a rules technicality was breached and the catcher was entitled to become a free agent. The same thing happened with Fred Lynn, but the Sox traded him before he went into free agency. Fisk put himself on the market and signed with the White Sox. And so the club lost the man who was perhaps the greatest catcher in their history, who had stroked their most dramatic home run, a man whose New

England heritage had made him seem the most Red Sox of Red Sox players.

The Red Sox won nothing in 1981, though they had two cracks at it because of the split season decreed after the strike. After finishing fifth in the first half, the club played better ball when action resumed after the settlement, ending up second, a game-and-a-half behind Milwaukee. The composite picture of the odd year showed Sox with a 59–49 record, in fifth place, but just 2½ behind Milwaukee which had the best overall record in the league.

The 1982 season started well for Houk's men, thanks largely to the major's adept handling of a well-stocked bullpen that included Clear, Stanley, lefty Tom Burgmeier, and rookie right-hander Luis Aponte. The club was at or near the top into July. But then gradually they snuggled into third place, watching the Brewers slug out a close-run division title over the Orioles. Boston ended up six behind, but ten ahead of the fifth-place Yankees, whatever consolation that brought.

There were some fine performances. Rookie Wade Boggs, getting a chance to play when Lansford was injured, batted .345, though without sufficient at bats to qualify for the batting title. Rice, solidly carrying on the tradition of left field greatness started by Williams in 1939 and brought forward by Yastrzemski, batted .310. Batting champion Lansford fell to .301. When Carney began talking big money for his approaching free agency in 1983, he was traded to Oakland in December for long-baller Tony Armas.

Going into their ninth decade, the Red Sox remain vibrant and youthful, because baseball teams do not age. The names and the faces may change, but the style of play follows the eternal rhythms of youth. Fenway Park has grown old around these eternally young men, and this is for the better, as it balances this vibrant youth with mellowed history. Summer days on a baseball diamond belong to the swift and the strong; into the sweet balmy nights go the shouts of history in the making, and when the crowd is gone and the game is done, the shouts drift into the Fenway shades and join all that have gone before. And what a procession it is!

Enshrined at Fenway, from grandstand's edge to the roots of each grassblade, are the stored radiance of treasured moments, of rallies and no-hitters, of home runs and errors, of pennants won and lost, of golden Octobers recorded in the scorebooks of antiquity: the feats of Smoky Joe Wood, of Speaker, Hooper, and Lewis; of the trim young pitcher named Ruth; of the mighty Foxx and the dourly proud Grove; of Cronin and Doerr and Pesky; of the batting elitist named Williams and the man known as Yaz; of Tiant and Lynn and Rice.

These and all of their teammates through the better part of a century now have given their partisans pride and joy and excitement, and disappointment and heartache too. The tides of the past have run to memory, and every spring the future awaits, in the shape of a bat, a ball, a glove.

Rookie Carl Yastrzemski in 1961.

Right-handed pitcher and basketball player: six-foot-eight Gene Conley pitched for the Red Sox from 1961 to 1963, winning 15 in 1962. He also played for the Boston Celtics during those years.

Don Schwall, Rookie of the Year in the American League in 1961. The big right-hander was 15–7 that year, 9–15 the next, and was then traded to Pittsburgh.

139

Eddie Bressoud, Boston's slick-fielding shortstop from 1962 to 1965. He batted .293 in 1964.

Left: Bill Monbouquette, Red Sox ace during the first half of the 1960s. The right-hander pitched for Boston from 1958 through 1965. He was a 20-game winner in 1963.

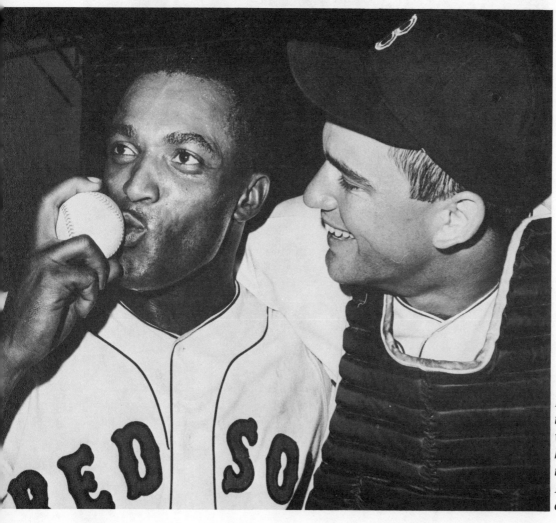

Earl Wilson kissing the baseball with which he completed his no-hitter against the Angels on June 26, 1962. With him is catcher Bob Tillman.

140

The Yastrzemski cut

Tony Conigliaro

Billy Herman

Dick Radatz

Rico Petrocelli. His 40 home runs in 1969 are the American League record for a shortstop.

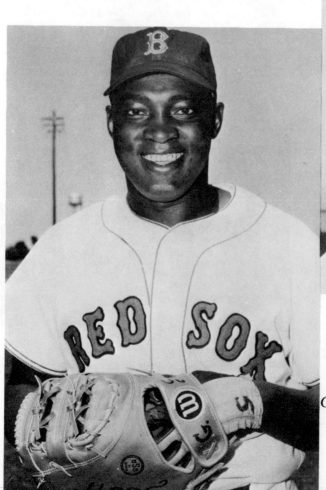

George Scott

Dick Williams

Dick Stuart

Billy Conigliaro, Tony's younger brother. Billy, an outfielder, was with the Red Sox from 1969 through 1971, and was then traded to Milwaukee.

The Red Sox got righty José Santiago from Kansas City in 1966. He was 12–4 in the pennant year of 1967, 9–4 the next year, and then hurt his arm.

Elston Howard

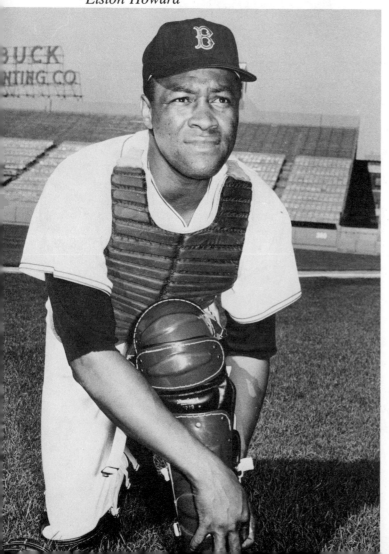

Jim Lonborg. He pitched for the Red Sox from 1965 through 1971, but was never the same after his skiing accident.

Ken Harrelson

Yastrzemski being greeted at home after putting one away at Yankee Stadium. That's Reggie Smith on the left and Mike Andrews.

Albert (Sparky) Lyle, Red Sox relief pitcher from 1967 through 1971, when he was traded to the Yankees for Danny Cater.

Below: Long-time White Sox ace Gary Peters joined the Red Sox in 1970. The southpaw worked the Fenway slab for three years, with a 16–11 record in 1971 his best showing.

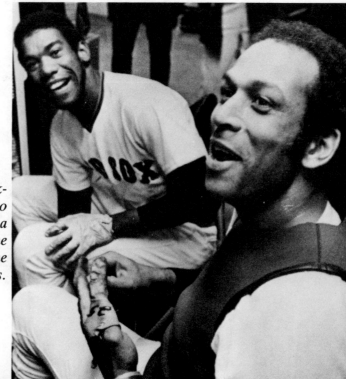

That's southpaw Roger Moret in the background listening to designated hitter Orlando Cepeda respond to a reporter's question after a game in April 1973. Cepeda played just one year for Boston, batting .289 with 20 home runs.

146

Obtained from the Cubs in 1968, right-hander Ray Culp gave the Red Sox some excellent years. He was 16–6 in 1968, 17–8 in 1969. He pitched for Boston until 1973.

Reggie Smith starred in the Red Sox outfield from 1966 through 1973. He hit over .300 three times for Boston, with a high of .309 in 1969. He was traded to the Cardinals in 1973 for Rick Wise and Bernie Carbo.

Mike Nagy, a tall right-hander who broke in with the Red Sox with a 12–2 record in 1969. He never repeated that success and left the club in 1972.

Manager Eddie Kasko having a look at short-stop Luis Aparicio's fractured finger in June 1972. Aparicio was the club's regular shortstop from 1971 through 1973.

At bat: Number 8.

Denny Doyle

Rick Burleson

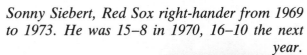

Sonny Siebert, Red Sox right-hander from 1969 to 1973. He was 15–8 in 1970, 16–10 the next year.

Darrell Johnson

149

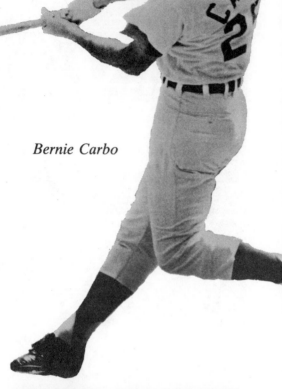

Bernie Carbo

Fred Lynn

Dwight Evans

Bill Lee

Dick Drago

Jim Rice looking one over.

151

Luis Tiant

Jim Rice

Ferguson Jenkins

Rick Wise

Fred Lynn striding into one.

The expression on Johnny Bench's face tells you what's about to happen. Fred Lynn, trying to score after tagging up on a fly ball in the sixth inning of the first game of the 1975 Series, is going to be out.

Carlton Fisk giving body English to his home run in the twelfth inning of the sixth game of the 1975 World Series.

Don Zimmer

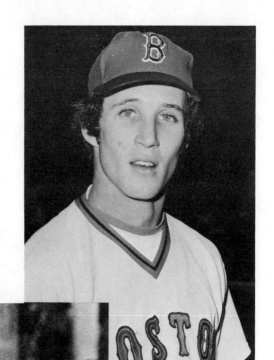

Butch Hobson

Bill Campbell

Carlton Fisk

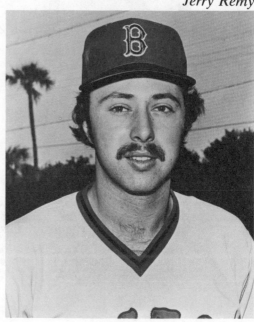

Fred Lynn

Mike Torrez

Jim Rice

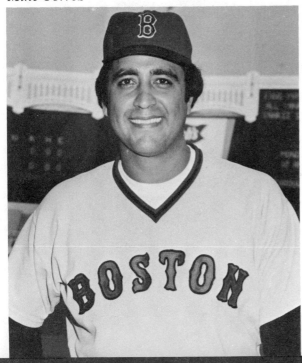

That's Butch Hobson sliding safely into home.
The catcher is Milwaukee's Charley Moore.

Dennis Eckersley giving it all he has.

Yastrzemski and Campbell

Carlton Fisk digging out a low one.

Bob Stanley

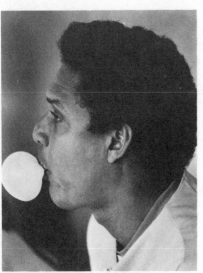

Tony Perez bubbling over.

Tom Burgmeier

Dave Stapleton

Cecil Cooper, who went to Milwaukee and made good.

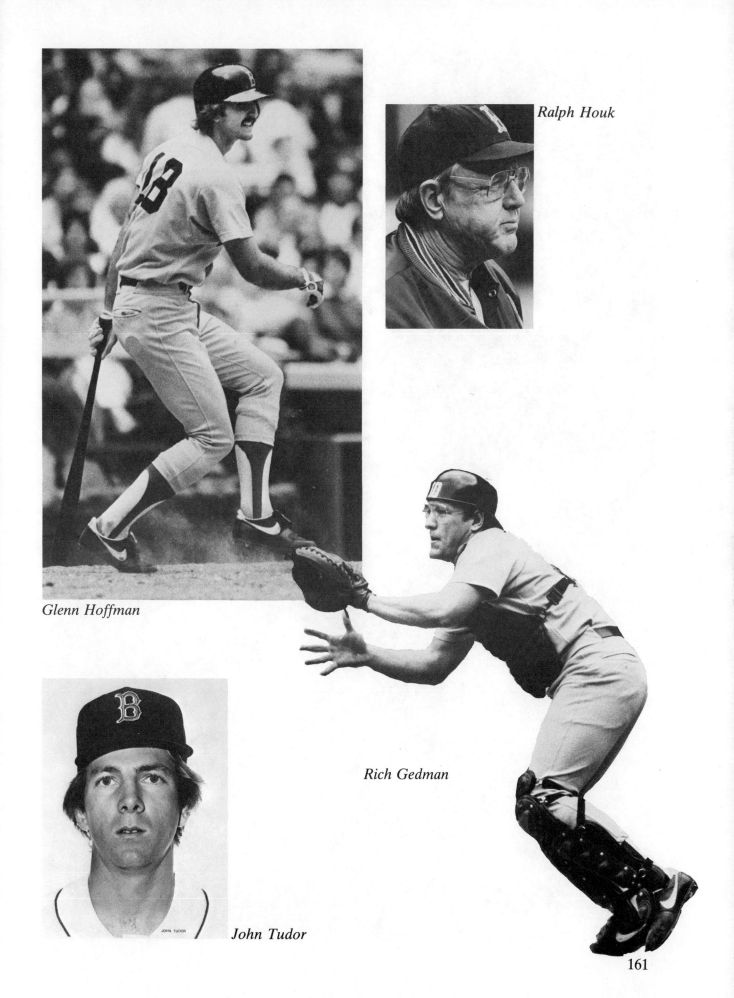

Ralph Houk

Glenn Hoffman

Rich Gedman

John Tudor

161

Carl Yastrzemski

162

Gary Allenson

Wade Boggs

Mark Clear

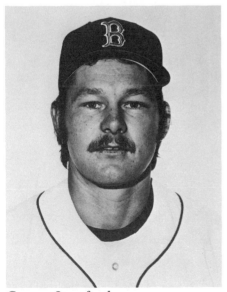

Carney Lansford

Fenway Park

Jim Rice

Right: The last farewell